Jean-Paul Viguier

Jean-Paul Viguier: Architecture 1992 – 2002

Philip Jodidio

Birkhäuser – Publishers for Architecture
Basel   Berlin   Boston

Book design: Binocular, New York

Translation of Selected Works and Biography:
Sarah Parsons, Paris

Cover photograph: Nicolas Borel (façade detail
of Cœur Défense Office Building)

A CIP catalogue record for this book is available
from the Library of Congress, Washington D.C., USA

Deutsche Bibliothek Cataloging-in-Publication Data

Viguier, Jean-Paul:
Jean-Paul Viguier : architecture 1992 – 2002 / Philip
Jodidio. – Basel ; Boston ; Berlin : Birkhäuser, 2002
    ISBN 3-7643-6500-5

© 2002 Birkhäuser – Publishers for Architecture
P.O. Box 133, CH-4010 Basel, Switzerland
A member of the BertelsmannSpringer Publishing Group

Printed on acid-free paper produced from
chlorine-free pulp. TCF ∞

Printed in Germany
ISBN 3-7643-6500-5

9 8 7 6 5 4 3 2 1

http://www.birkhauser.ch

Frontispiece:
Façade and atrium detail, Cœur Défense, Paris.

Contents

Rigor and intellectual honesty are two of the most evident qualities of Jean-Paul Viguier. Influenced by modern masters like Ludwig Mies van der Rohe, he has carved out a unique place in the world of French contemporary architecture, working in both private and the public spheres. Indeed, most of his colleagues concentrate in one or the other of these sectors, creating a division that Viguier has been one of the few to successfully bridge in recent years. In his mind, and in his work, these characteristics are closely related to a strict sense of architectural geometry. The architect does not eschew repetitive forms, using them to emphasize a horizontal continuity, a smoothness (*lisse*) that often cedes to generous, relatively complex interior spaces. The atrium, a favored device of Jean-Paul Viguier, is a gathering place, a symbolic glass heart that signals an openness that may not be readily evident from his "smooth" exterior cladding. Despite his Modernist penchants, Viguier frequently criss-crosses his vast interiors with multiple bridges that bring Piranesi to mind more than Mies. There is a vertiginous emptiness to some Viguier interiors, coupled with a sure sense of the possibilities of his construction materials, that may reveal an almost hidden desire to "transgress" the strict regularity of his chosen vocabulary. As an architect who is clearly fascinated by engineering, he looks to other areas like airplane design for some of his inspiration, and he has occasionally shown interest in bridge construction. Jean-Paul Viguier muses on his own strict regularity as an architect, alternating between criticism of more "artistic" colleagues, and what might appear to be a certain jealousy of their freedom. Just as he manages equilibrium between public and private work, he would like also to walk the fine line that divides responsibility from creativity. Although one obviously does not exclude the other, finding the proper balance seems to be an issue that is at the heart of Viguier's work.

Born in 1946, the son of a Toulouse architect, his earliest sources of inspiration were decidedly Modernist. As he says, "my father brought me to Paris in 1962 or 1963 and we visited the Unesco building by Marcel Breuer, Pier Luigi Nervi and Bernard Zehrfuss. The equilibrium and modernity of that building astonished me. It was above and beyond what I could imagine the future would look like. I would have liked to design it myself. It was subsequent to that visit that I decided to study architecture at the Beaux-Arts." It might be noted that with Nervi's auditorium, the Unesco Headquarters from the outset did not have the kind of absolute Modernist purity that figures such as Mies van der Rohe sought and obtained from buildings like the Seagram Tower on Park Avenue in New York. Unesco was already a kind of hybrid between the nature-oriented engineering of Nervi and the more brutal Modernism of a figure like Breuer. In his admiration for the Unesco Headquarters, in his somewhat premature desire to have wanted to build something of the kind, Jean-Paul Viguier exhibited a precocious complexity in his role-models that was later reflected in his own architecture.

Viguier's stay at the Beaux-Arts was eventful, if for no other reason than that it coincided with the upheavals of 1968. But he also brought a typically willful attitude to his own studies—one that was indicative of his future career. Assigned to the atelier of the architect Eugène Beaudoin, he was astonished not to have been required to study the real urban environment. "What I wanted above all was to be able to imagine working on the bits and pieces that make up the city — housing, public space, or offices. In the six years I spent at the École des Beaux-Arts I never once worked on housing — the only thing that interested the School at that time was monumental architecture." Beyond these failings, the Beaux-Arts was not far from the center of the 1968 Parisian revolts, a fact that led the French administration to seek to empty its ranks as quickly as possible. "The instructions received from the administration," says Jean-Paul Viguier, "were that any student who had reached the level of studies where I was at the time should simply receive a diploma. They really wanted to get rid of us! I couldn't stand this lack of respect, so with a group of friends we went to seek out the architects Jean Bossu, Georges-Henri Pingusson, and Miroslav Kostanjevac. With them we created a new study unit called UP5 (Unité Pédagogique 5) which was set up in the Grand Palais in Paris."

Viguier's professors at UP5 had a decided influence on him. He says, "Bossu was my only real teacher in architecture. He was an exceptional character — he had worked for several years with Le Corbusier in the rue de Sèvres atelier. Mr. Kostanjevac was my professor for construction. He had worked with Pier Luigi Nervi on the Unesco auditorium. He taught me the importance of materials and the constraints they impose on architecture. With him, I learned that a building has to stand up, to last, but that it must also be beautiful. He showed me how creativity can impose itself on materials by placing them in new situations." It is interesting that Viguier chooses to emphasize almost equally teachers who were interested in architecture on the one hand and engineering on the other, as though the two could not readily be separated. In fact, Jean-Paul Viguier is one of the contemporary

Façade and window detail, Gaz de France, La Plaine Saint-Denis.

architects who has the most feeling for the art of engineering.

Though interesting, Jean-Paul Viguier's experience to this point did little to distinguish him from other rising architects of his age. He readily admits that the United States brought a new dimension to his understanding of his chosen field. "In 1967, I spent three months in New York, and there, in front of the Ford Foundation, I felt the same kind of emotion I had had when I first saw the Unesco building." Kevin Roche's seminal Ford Foundation headquarters is one of the best-known post-War buildings. For Viguier, its vast atrium, enclosing a veritable forest, was an essential discovery. With this one, spectacular gesture, Roche brought nature into the heart of the city, and created a sense of common space, whereas most modern office buildings did quite the contrary, emphasizing anonymity and distance from nature. It might be noted that the Ford Foundation exhibits its glass atrium

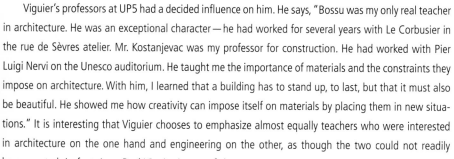

Gaz de France Research Center, La Plaine Saint-Denis, France, 1981-86 This complex project was intended to reunite the laboratories and facilities for group personnel of the natural gas company Gaz de France in a single location, whereas they had previously been spread throughout the Paris region. A total of twenty thousand square meters of floor space were created on a seven-hectare plot of land just outside of the city. The complex is organized like a university campus and includes thirteen thousand five hundred square maters of offices and computer facilities; as well as experimental laboratories, storage facilities, ateliers and a five thousand square meter restaurant. The white tonalities of the architecture are intended to encourage research and to contrast with the garden atmosphere of the Center. A seven-story laboratory tower emerges above a u-shaped building housing the administration, research and computer facilities.

openly toward the street — proposing a kind of symbiosis with its environment that is infrequent in Viguier's work. Other work by Kevin Roche, such as his extensions to the Metropolitan Museum of Art, with their frequent atrium-like spaces do emphasize a certain continuity with the sources of Jean-Paul Viguier's designs.

In 1971, Jean-Paul Viguier obtained a scholarship to attend the Harvard Graduate School of Design. Although Walter Gropius was by that time no longer the head of the GSD, his influence was still very present in Cambridge. Viguier saw others, like I.M. Pei who made brief appearances at the GSD, but what he retained above all was the influence of Mies, as it was expressed in the United States. "After a moment spent admiring Frank Lloyd Wright," says Viguier, "and despite his feeling for form, his talent for drawing, and his obvious contribution as a great architect, I turned more towards the founder of modern architecture. He was incomparable in his sober abstraction, always working on the sharp edge which distinguishes great architecture from nothing at all. He knew how to impose his will on materials. He smoked Havana cigars. He said 'Less is more,' and 'God is in the details.' Mies van der Rohe too came from the Bauhaus. He was a Master, which is to say an architect who changes the order of things."

Back in France, Jean-Paul Viguier managed very quickly to work on one of the areas for which he has the most affection, that of housing. Typically centralized, the French government decided on the construction of a series of "new towns" (villes nouvelles). Although qualified architects were frequently called on for the design of these new towns, there was little overriding sense of urban order, and each participant tended to think up his own scheme. Viguier's contribution to this often dissonant campaign began with Cergy Pontoise where he built four hundred-fifty welfare apartments in 1976 (Les Linandes). As he says, "then I built a university residence in Évry (1978); housing in Saint-Quentin-en-Yvelines (Quartier de la Gare, 1983); an RER station in Marne-la-Vallée (Euro-Disneyland, Chessy, 1989) and a hotel for Disney (Hotel Cheyenne, preliminary design by Robert A.M. Stern, 1990)." His work in this context continues with the shopping center he is designing for the new town of Sénart.

In France, public projects are given to architects almost entirely on the basis of competitions. Jean-Paul Viguier is a veteran of numerous competitions. Despite frequent participation and a reasonably successful series of efforts, Viguier did not manage to win any of the major competitions launched under the presidency of François Mitterrand, and known in France collectively as the "Grands Travaux." A first prize jury winner for the Opéra Bastille and Défense competitions, he saw the Uruguayan-Canadian architect Carlos Ott win the first and the Danish designer Otto Spreckelsen take the second. "After the Défense competition," says Viguier, "François Mitterrand told me that he had not really understood my design. He apparently preferred a more literary project, one that could be described as an 'arch of humanity, a link between peoples', as Spreckelsen had called his project." A hint of bitterness, including occasional references to the high numbers of foreign architects selected during this period characterize Jean-Paul Viguier's declarations on the subject of the "Grands Travaux." He was nonetheless a winner in numerous other important competitions including that for the French Pavilion in Seville (1990) and the Pont du Gard (1991). He also participated unsuccessfully in competitions for the International Conference Center in Paris (1990, won by Francis Soler and never built); the Congress Center at the Porte Maillot in Paris (1994, won by Christian de Portzamparc); and the football Stadium in Saint-Denis built for the World Cup Soccer Championship (1994, competition won by Jean Nouvel, project built by another group including Michel Macary).

In 1992, Jean-Paul Viguier took an important decision in his career — that of separating from his long-time associate Jean-François Jodry. His description of this separation is significant in terms of understanding his entire body of work since 1992. It might be said that the direction he struck out on following the creation of his own office in 1992 was already very much on his mind several years earlier. He and his associate worked at the same time on two projects, one of which was more carefully and slowly designed than the other. The Gaz de France building (Saint-Denis, 1985) and Métropole 19 (1986), a twenty thousand square meter industrial office building located on the rue d'Aubervilliers in Paris were finished almost simultaneously. "I was working on both of these buildings at the same time," says Viguier, "Gaz de France was a complicated, slow and very difficult to put together. Métropole 19 was the exact opposite. We did that project in three months, and built it in six. There was a very powerful thrust in Métropole 19 that lead me to think carefully about my whole way of working. We won the prestigious Équerre d'argent prize (special mention), not for Gaz de France, but for Métropole 19. That in itself was a revelation to me. We worked under stress with prefabricated elements in one case and with a complex design process in the other — surprisingly, it was the rapid track that brought us much closer to success than the slow careful one."

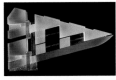

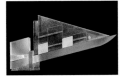

Jean-Paul Viguier's statements on the comparative success of the Métropole 19 and Gaz de France go even further into a kind of self-psychoanalysis that again reveals a great deal about his ambitions, and his perceived failings. "I have this good boy, or good student side to me, always first in my class. I have lived with a kind of absolute sense of moral obligation to do things well. When we designed the Gaz de France headquarters, I applied myself, in that spirit of finishing every last detail to perfection and along came this other project, Métropole 19, that had its own fast-track logic. There was clearly something to be learned for me in this difference, in the beneficial side to doing things fast and hard."

"One of the reasons that I abandoned my partnership with Jean-François Jodry," says Jean-Paul Viguier, "was that as far as I was concerned, the office had become too big. At that time, even more so than today, there was a clear division between the architects in France who do public work and the ones who seek private projects. Maybe it was my 'American' culture that influenced me," continues Viguier, "but I could never see any real difference between the two. Of course in France, there is an ideological background to this debate, that I never really felt concerned by. I always wanted to balance public and private commissions. Some people certainly feel that there is a kind of facility or a seduction in the private work, as though private work is easier. After the French Pavilion for Seville, our office almost literally exploded because we had so much work to do. We had forty-five to fifty projects going simultaneously and one hundred fifty people working for us. This happened without either my associate or myself really wanting such a result, but Jean-François Jodry went more in that direction than I cared to. There were even projects that got built by our office that I never saw until they were finished. I no longer had direct contact with my own staff."

Progressive views of the assembly of the model for France Télévision showing the main sections of the building.

It was the tendency to an almost industrial approach to architecture that Jean-Paul Viguier, to his credit, rejected in separating from Jean-François Jodry. "I decided I wanted a smaller office," says Viguier, "undoubtedly one focussing more on an artisan's approach to architecture." Despite his notion of a less industrial approach, Jean-Paul Viguier is undeniably an architect who is interested in large-scale designs. He has almost never built on a small scale, having designed only one private house, for example. He emphasizes that social housing is a much less repetitive form of design than is creating an office building. Others might well find that apartment design, despite the various types and variants involved, is already a highly repetitive form of architecture. "I am comfortable with repetition," admits Viguier, "it is the tradition of the Bauhaus that I love. The art of perspective, the art of rational drawing, a certain rigor in the approach, are my ways of approaching architecture. A logical explanation follows the development of architecture step by step, rather than an intuitive justification," he concludes. Viguier's emphasis on logic as opposed to intuition is a central factor in his architecture, an explanation for his strengths and perhaps for some of his weaknesses as well.

The visible calmness and openness of Jean-Paul Viguier's own offices may be one of the most visible proofs that his separation from Jodry has permitted him to give the kind of attention to each project that he was unable to provide in the context of his partnership. There is an almost familial atmosphere in the office of Viguier, a fact that is highlighted by the presence of his wife Annie, who has a complete mastery over the careful documentation associated with each project. Indeed in her work, the rigor and logic of architecture that are leitmotifs of Jean-Paul Viguier find their visual and written counterparts. Few architectural offices are as well provided for in terms of their available photographs, drawings and press clippings.

Metal components designed for integration into the pre-stressed concrete, Métropole 19, Paris.

The French Pavilion in Seville is another particularly revealing case in terms of Jean-Paul Viguier's approach to architecture. "In a way," he says, "the French Pavilion took the idea of abstraction as far as it could go while still serving some discernable function." Essentially made up of a cubic hole in the ground, an open square and a suspended "sky" or covering above, the design was controversial and problematic to build. "François Seigneur was a member of the team, and to say that we fought like cats and dogs might not be an exaggeration," says Jean-Paul Viguier. "He behaved like an artist, and we did not get along. Construction hardly interested him at all, he had a kind of painterly vision of the Pavilion. My own inhibitions as an architect, my need to make things work, made it difficult for me to follow him in his apparent need to transgress what I feel are our

Métropole 19 Building, Paris, France, 1986–88
Housed in two parallel five story buildings, respectively twenty and sixteen meters thick, running parallel to the rue d'Aubervilliers , this twenty-two thousand meter complex with six thousand square meters of parking space, was built with prefabricated floor slabs and pre-stressed beams. The load-bearing walls were also prefabricated and are clad in brick veneer panels. Construction cost was sixty million francs or 2,727 francs per square meter. The construction was carried out between June 1987 and May 1988. Jean-Paul Viguier cites the rapid design and construction process of this industrial building as an example as to what his office was capable of doing under difficult conditions, as opposed to the long preparation that went into the Gaz de France laboratories. Métropole 19 won the 1988 Équerre d'argent prize (special mention) given by France's construction magazine Le Moniteur.

professional obligations." Indeed, François Seigneur, a former partner of Jean Nouvel, did play an important role in making the French Pavilion one of the most spectacularly minimal and abstract projects associated with Jean-Paul Viguier. He rightfully sees his own contribution in terms of designing the "sky" or the pillars that hold it up in such a way as to permit them to be solid and yet appear to be almost insubstantial in their physical presence.

The questions of "artistic" content and what he calls "transgression" obviously preoccupy Jean-Paul Viguier, and he is quite open in discussing this important issue in his work. "Obviously there is an artistic dimension in architecture in the sense that every project is a unique act of creation. Paul Valéry wrote that the soul needs beauty, the body what is useful or comfortable, and society needs what is durable. For me, those are the three aspects of architecture and they cannot be separated." From this almost indisputable premise Jean-Paul Viguier goes on to mention his own doubts. "The architect is confronted with the permanent temptation of transgression, which is to say, art. Art is form of continual transgression. We seek to go beyond established limits, to find a way to invent the new. That search is necessary for art and dangerous for architecture. We must try to make materials do more and more, to push glass for example to its structural limits. My idea of smoothness requires me to push construction materials to the utmost, but glass can't break, it must last thirty years." It is interesting to note that Jean-Paul Viguier's analysis of the artistic content of architecture quickly branches out into the subject of technical factors such as the breaking point of glass. Smoothness, like a taut skin, is in both the real and the philosophical senses, the envelope within which architecture must be contained. Just as Jean-Paul Viguier states that glass can be pushed to its limits but must not break, so too he feels that the artistic or "intuitive" content of a building must be contained within its metaphorical skin. The glass must not break and the artistic content cannot reach the point of "transgression."

It would seem worthwhile nonetheless to pursue the issue of Jean-Paul Viguier's approach to the esthetic content of his own work. "I have a kind of self-imposed restraint," he admits. When I create forms, I make semi-circles. I am committed to Euclidean geometry. I always seek to remain in a rational order of things, one that I can explain. I worked with Frank Gehry on the Euro-Disney project. He made balls out of sheets of paper and splattered them with plaster. Afterwards, he had someone in his studio make wooden models on that basis. That is a type of creativity that I am not at all at ease with. Don't get me wrong, I admire it, I find it magnificent, but I just don't know how to work like that." Even the casual listener might well find a pointed irony in Jean-Paul Viguier's description of Gehry's work. No, he doesn't know how to work like Frank Gehry, and no, he doesn't want to learn. For Viguier, Gehry's work is exactly the kind of artistic or intuitive transgression that he seeks to avoid.

Called on to cite works of art that he admires, Jean-Paul Viguier gives the examples of Mark Rothko's painting or that of the Blue Rider group. It might be considered interesting that both Kandinsky and Rothko were of Russian origin, and undoubtedly given to a more emotional approach than their French counterparts, for example. Both too experimented with the fine line dividing order from chaos. Kandinsky and the Blue Rider were firmly situated at the origins of abstract art, the point in which the figurative image of the rider dissolved into the emotions and inner feelings that suffused early abstraction. Rothko, with his shimmering fields of color, was continually on the fine edge between landscape and mental abstraction, between strict order and the blackness of the abyss. The rigor and strength of Kandinsky and Rothko, their willful experimentation with the breaking points of the history of art might be seen as models for Viguier's own thoughts about his work. He too seeks the point of division between the order of architecture and the "transgression" of art, between durability and the breaking point of construction materials. Obviously he grants a greater freedom to painters than to architects, who are bound in his mind to make things that will "stand up," a requirement that artists can ignore if they wish.

Three projects that Jean-Paul Viguier has worked on in recent years have left a recognizable mark on the west of Paris. The first of these is the André Citroën Park, located on the grounds of the former Citroën automobile factories, next to Richard Meier's Canal Plus building. In an unusual arrangement, Viguier (who was at the time still associated with Jodry) split work on this entirely new fourteen-hectare park with another architect, Patrick Berger and with two landscape architects, Alain Provost and Gilles Clément. This division of responsibility was a result of the initial 1985 competition in which each architect had been associated with a landscape architect (Viguier with Provost and Berger with Clément), and in which it was decided that four heads would be better than one. With its powerful lines and contrasting spaces, varying between an empty central rectangle and more densely planted and designed edges, the André Citroën park does not appear to suffer from the multiplicity of creative talents involved. Viguier affirmed his own presence in this very successful park by subsequently designing a railroad viaduct and the areas near the Seine. The long white arch of the viaduct is indeed the visible sign of the presence of the park from the opposite bank of the Seine, or from the river itself.

Also very visible from the Seine and located nearby, the headquarters of France Télévision is one of Jean-Paul Viguier's most significant projects. Aside from it's physical location, the very fact of designing headquarters for the national television stations France 2 and France 3 placed the architect in a rather exposed situation. An underlying fact of the project is that the respective staffs of the stations do not get along, and that one of them (France 2) is far bigger than the other one. Thus, within a single building, housing relatively complex facilities such as the recording studios, it was necessary to create a kind of duality to compensate for the preponderance of one entity vis-à-vis the other. As is often the case, Viguier was concerned here with the issue of "transgression". "When you participate in a competition," he says, "there is a kind of solitude that pushes you towards transgression because there is nobody opposite you. In the case of France Télévision, the contact with Jean-Pierre Elkabbach was essential." President of the French national television networks, Elkabbach is very well known figure in France, having previously been a noted news presenter and political interviewer. Despite its strongly horizontal lines, the France Télévision building has a somewhat irregular pattern in its white marble façade cladding. This "artistic" touch is the result of the talks between Viguier and Elkabbach. "He absolutely wanted the architecture to tell a story," says Jean-Paul Viguier, "so I made up this idea of the pixels on a screen fading out." Though this source of inspiration is not readily apparent from the building's actual façade, the idea satisfied Jean-Pierre Elkabbach, and left the architect somewhat less pleased. "I regret getting involved in this kind of story-telling that is fundamentally opposed to the sort of rigor that I aspire to," he concludes.

In its riverside setting, closely bound by rail lines and large roads, the France Télévision building does mark a sort of entrance to the French capital. In this respect, like the nearby arch of the André Citroën viaduct it signals the success of Jean-Paul Viguier as one of those who has fashioned some of the most visible aspects of Paris. Within, France Télévision tells a somewhat different story, if only because of its fundamental, inherent division between rival networks. The long corridors and partially underground recording studios do not necessarily make for luminous working space, but the entrance atrium of the building, stretching up through its full height, does emphasize the common goals and duties of the persons who work in this structure. Jean-Paul Viguier does point out to visitors that it is his technical mastery of construction techniques that has allowed the construction of the recording studios in relatively close proximity to train lines. Both vibration and sound levels have been kept to acceptable levels through devices that he conceived. Far above these "black boxes", the atrium in its uppermost level, takes on a rough technical kind of quality, or a Piranesian complexity that seems to be the counterpart of the "smoothness" so avidly sought out by Jean-Paul Viguier in façade cladding, for example. The executive offices benefit from open views onto the Seine, but many other spaces give an impression of being rather closed.

This building, though undeniably modern in its plan and construction emphasizes an underlying duality in Jean-Paul Viguier's work, a "Frenchness" that undoubtedly distinguishes his work from that of the Bauhaus masters, for example. Though the stark geometry of Miesian buildings may lie concealed somewhere in the background of the France Télévision headquarters, it is a complex structure that reveals not only a desire to tell a story but also a need to accommodate client needs to such an extent that it becomes evident that there are divisions within the organization concerned. The "less is more" of Mies here moves towards a kind of sophistication and complexity that surely bears some relationship to the spirit of modern France. When Jean-Paul Viguier evoked the apparently large number of commissions given to foreign architects under the banner of François Mitterrand's Grands Travaux, he was in a way pleading for the presence of a "national" character in architecture, a "Frenchness" that the France Télévision building amply displays.

An exterior view of the C3D Headquarters, Boulogne-Billancourt.

C3D Headquarters, Boulogne-Billancourt, France, 1989 – 92 This twenty thousand meter headquarters building for a French banking group is set on nine floors in a square layout surrounding a central atrium. Four hundred seventy five parking spots are available on three underground levels. Conference rooms, a restaurant and a café are situated on the ground floor, near the one thousand square meter atrium. The idea of placing the restaurant in such a preferential location participates in Viguier's idea that the atrium is the focal point of the building. Clad in blue Lanheilin granite, the building stands out from its environment near the Porte Saint Cloud because of its monolithic cubical structure, and because of its visible dome, covering the central atrium. Heat pumps are used in order to minimize energy consumption in this building. The total budget for the project was two hundred forty million Francs.

Despite his break with Jean-François Jodry, Jean-Paul Viguier's preference for the design of large buildings has continued unabated. One of his largest projects has just been completed in the Défense area of Paris. The so-called Cœur Défense complex is made up of two thirty nine-story towers, and three eight story blocks, the whole connected by a vast atrium. From the Ford Foundation to the hotel architecture of figures like John Portman, this presence of the atrium in Jean-Paul Viguier's work would seem to have been influenced by the example of post-war American architecture. In the case of the Cœur Défense, the large-scale is also indicative of Jean-Paul Viguier's fascination with the technological means necessary to achieve architectural ends. In this respect, his thinking approaches that of rare engineer-architects like Pier Luigi Nervi whom he clearly admired. "We conceived those towers at the Défense like a piece of civil engineering," he declares proudly, "we used bridge design to create the vast atrium spaces."

Staggered, one a bit behind the other, the rounded Cœur Défense towers stand out from their relatively undistinguished architectural background. They are visible both from the central areas of the Défense, and from the boulevard that enters the area, in the axis of the Champs-Élysées. Set on the site of the former Esso building, this project had the added impetus of representing a second generation of tower on the same piece of land, a kind of challenge to the architect to show that tall building design has actually made progress since the 1960's.

Working with his usual notion of repetition, tempered by a desire to create somewhat less regular patterns, Jean-Paul Viguier designed an innovative system for the sunshades in the Cœur Défense towers. Using double-glazing, the architect left a large enough gap to insert sunshades that automatically change the aspect of the towers as the sun turns around them. It should be noted that one of Viguier's steadfast principles is that glass is to be used for windows only. "The presence of glass must be the sign of the presence of a window," he declares. "Glass is transparent, and that is a fact that we cannot toy with," he concludes solemnly. With a combination of their automatic movement and the less predictable decisions of the inhabitant of each office, the towers take on an almost infinite variety of appearances, varying from a high level of transparency to a complete opacity. Indeed when all of the shades are closed, the buildings seem like sculpted white masses with no apparent windows.

In the Cœur Défense, as in many of his other buildings, Jean-Paul Viguier uses the atrium as a unifying device, a physical and symbolic reminder that despite the large numbers of offices that make up a complex like this one, the people who work in them can meet, and can above all be reminded that they are part of a coherent architectural whole. This is a space that reveals its creator's penchant for exploring the limits of materials and the possibilities offered by engineering solutions. Unlike the anthropomorphic or nature-oriented inspiration that often underlies the work of true engineer architects like Nervi or Santiago Calatrava, Viguier remains in the register of geometric modernism, and does not seek out an impression of extreme lightness, for example. A Viguier building is meant to last, and it shows. The Cœur Défense atrium has more to do with bridge design than it does with a metaphoric bubble. Buckminster Fuller has not visited the thought that went into this space.

Like some other figures who are fascinated by technology, such as Lord Norman Foster, Jean-Paul Viguier admits that he is "a thief of images, like all architects." His source material however, would not appear to be the work of his colleagues, whom he rarely includes in his circle of friends. "I would rather go to an air show like the one held each year at the Bourget Airport," he says, "than to go to a construction fair". "I look carefully at the design not only of airplanes, but also at that of household items that are often very innovative," he continues.

When he is asked if the lessons learned in the comparison of his Métropole 19 and Gaz de France projects have really been applied elsewhere, Jean-Paul Viguier points to one of his most recent large buildings, a four hundred sixteen room hotel designed for the French Accor chain in the heart of Chicago. Here, in the birthplace of the skyscraper, a city marked by Wright and Mies as well, Viguier obviously had a point to prove — that it is possible to design a tower that differs from its neighbors, and still fulfills its client's requirements. By accentuating one angle of the tower, thus making it lean forward, and selecting a light-colored cladding, he has succeeded in making this Sofitel Hotel stand out in the immediate vicinity of the massive John Hancock Tower. With his usual predilection for "smooth" horizontal cladding, Viguier also creates a counterpoint to the vertical thrust of the tower.

There is a public perception in France that engineering and architecture are professions that are often at odds. This may be due to the time-honored system of the so-called "Grandes écoles" — the elite schools that form the country's leaders. The best-known engineering school in France, the École nationale des Ponts et Chaussées is one of those, and its graduates are granted a respect that is not always given to architects. Badly shaken by the very events surrounding the social upheavals of 1968 that disturbed Viguier's university years, the system of architectural education in France is by no means as elitist as that of the engineering profession. This is not to say that France is without its own group of "star" architects, like the Pritzker Prize winner Christian de Portzamparc or Jean Nouvel, but on the whole it may be that architects are not generally perceived in France as being significant public figures, as they are in many other countries. Perhaps because of his own interest in engineering, Jean-Paul Viguier feels that, on the contrary, there is a real, efficient dialogue in France between these two intermingled aspects of the art of building. He is unexpectedly critical of what he perceives to be a much more difficult situation in the United States, where his Chicago project has left him with a distinct feeling that architects and engineers cooperate far less in the America than they do in France.

Above, four construction views of the French Pavilion for Expo '92, Seville, Spain. The excavation was intended for a very large screen, set horizontally below the square formed by the elevated canopy.

Although he has left his mark more than anywhere else in the area of large buildings, Jean-Paul Viguier has also shown a great interest in landscape architecture and site development. The most significant recent example of his skill in this area is his work on the Pont du Gard, subsequent to a 1991 competition that he won. Here, he not only designed the requisite facilities for arriving tourists, but he managed to clear the areas immediately around the famous aqueduct so that visitors discover the monument in the kind of splendid isolation in which it was originally conceived. In this instance, his work shows a subtle blend of respect for an historic monument and an acute awareness of the need to bring a modern approach to such a heavily visited tourist site. Jean-Paul Viguier played a significant role in the decision to ask the American artist James Turrell to light the aqueduct. Turrell's intervention did provoke negative reactions from a part of France's protective cultural establishment, but it showed Viguier at his best, daring to allow art to play a role in the public perception of architecture. Jean-Paul Viguier readily cites James Turrell's work with light when asked which works of art he admires most. He also cites the wrapping of the Reichstag by Christo and Jeanne-Claude, another case of interaction between art and architecture or art and urban space.

Jean-Paul Viguier has not been a stranger to controversy in his recent work, and the relationship of the modern to the traditional, always complex in France, has been a source of difficulty for him. It is just opposite the Cathedral of Reims that he was called on to build a "Médiatheque", the modern French cousin of the more traditional public library. Viguier was criticized both for designing a rather strict modern block for the corner opposite the church, and for his decision to rehabilitate an undistinguished

neighboring 19th century police headquarters as part of his project. When questioned about these decisions, he made it clear that a modern architect could not be called on to create a pastiche of the Gothic
or any other period. As far as the police building is concerned, he defended his position by recalling that
much of the city had been destroyed during the war, and that there was no point in his mind to further
accentuate the loss of memory imposed by the bombs. A high base made of local stone further contributed
to controversy although it was intended as a bow to traditions of the region.

"Today," says Jean-Paul Viguier, "much more than in the time of Mies, architects are the product of
a cultural blending so that their point of view is much broader." Indeed, in comparing the work of Viguier
to that of the Bauhaus masters for example, an obvious fact strikes the observer. Whereas pure Modernism
often rejected the need to respond to its immediate environment, instead creating free-standing master-
pieces like the Villa Savoye or the Barcelona Pavilion, Viguier's brand of modern architecture does involve
the kind of reactive design seen in Reims or at the Défense, for example. There is most certainly a geometric
bias in the basic designs of Viguier, but above and beyond that point, the use of engineering principles
and vertiginous atrium spaces complicates and enriches his approach.

Esso Headquarters, Rueil-
Malmaison. Three drawings
showing the mechanized
roof on the terrace in closed,
semi-open and open positions.

Other current work of the office of Jean-Paul Viguier includes entirely new construction, as is the case
of the very large Carré Sénart shopping center with over one hundred thousand square meters of retail
space and a seventeen-theater cinema multiplex; or the so-called "Ilôt M7" in the thirteenth arrondissement of Paris near the French National Library. The M7 project is
a fifty thousand square meter complex including offices and retail
space, set above an existing high-speed public transport facility (RER
Météor). He has also undertaken the restructuring of the Toulouse
Museum of Natural History, renovating twenty-five hundred square
meters of existing facilities, adding thirty-three hundred more, and tak-
ing on the design of a botanical garden (again with Alain Provost), as
well as the internal museum design. This series of new projects shows
the breadth of the capacities of Viguier's office, and involves both
purely commercial work such as the Carré Sénart, and public work
being carried out as a result of a competition won by the architect.
Amongst contemporary French architects, Jean-Paul Viguier may be
unique in his mastery of such a wide variety of types of work, and in
the fact that clients rely on him for everything from office towers to
botanical gardens.

Esso Headquarters, Rueil-Malmaison, France,
1990 – 92 Built for a two hundred million Franc
budget (1990 values), this project includes two buildings set in an "L" shape — the larger on nine stories,
and the smaller on eight. Two different types of
façade were chosen according to the environment —
a heavier, concrete and blue granite cladding near a
roadway, and a lighter glass and aluminum one near
the garden and the Seine River. The generous full-
height entrance hall is located on the north side. In the
larger wing, on the Seine side, a restaurant is located
on the garden and Seine side, computer facilities on
the second floor, and on the top floor, the offices of the
President and directors of the firm. In the smaller wing,
there is a fitness center and a medical facility for the
personnel, and on the eight floor, a terrace and a one-
hundred fifty seat auditorium. The whole is set around
a central garden, with weeping willows and other
vegetation typical near the banks of the Seine.

It might said that the architecture of Jean-Paul Viguier corresponds in an almost visible sense to
his own personality. His strong insistence on the *lisse* or smoothness of his cladding, coupled with the
notion that glass must be used only where there are actual windows, corresponds to his intellectual and
professional rigor, his "good student" approach. The uncompromising nature of his stances in these areas
does recall the tough purity of the Modernists. The rigor of Jean-Paul Viguier's stances on cladding

or façade design also betrays his interest in materials and their capacities. For the Cœur Défense, his sophisticated double-glazing minimizes heat gain, while providing a solution for sun shading, and consequently for the aesthetic appearance of the completed towers. The irregular patterns and play on opacity and transparency offered by the sun screens is the result of engineering solutions rather than a conscious "artistic" element of the design. Here "art" follows what is practical. Though it is not denied, it is placed in the secondary role where, according to Jean-Paul Viguier, it must remain—failing which he would delve into the realm of the "transgression" that he rejects.

Inside of Jean-Paul Viguier's buildings, a certain number of guiding principles are at work as well, but they do not give the same kind of "smooth" results he calls for in cladding. One consistent element of his work is his respect for the needs of the client, as evidenced, for example, in the complex duality of the France Télévision Headquarters. Another principle, seen frequently in his office buildings, is the use of the atrium as a binding, convivial factor. Undoubtedly influenced by his experience with American architecture, this presence of the atrium also brings to mind his interest in allowing some connection between nature and otherwise relatively cold materials and spaces. Within a building like France Télévision, the atrium that slices through the structure at the entrance does assume a kind of complexity, as it rises through the stories, that seems almost to be at odds with the idea of smoothness of the façades. Just under the glass at the top of the atrium, construction materials are displayed in an almost rough state, as though the architect was determined to show that "smoothness" is not all there is to a building.

Jean-Paul Viguier's frequent reference to the idea of artistic "transgression" in architecture is another key element in understanding his work. His admitted disputes with François Seigneur over the design of the French Pavilion in Seville, his somewhat ironic respect for Frank Gehry and his affirmation that he learned from the success of Métropole 19 are all indicative of what he perceives as an inherent conflict between the principles of architecture and the demands of artistic expression. Jean-Paul Viguier sees a similarity between art and architecture in that each produces unique objects, and yet his own admittedly geometric and repetitive designs aim more to solve practical problems than to create works of art. Jean-Paul Viguier labels art, in the sense of François Seigneur's "painterly" attitude, or Frank Gehry's sculptural approach, a "danger" for architecture. Buildings are meant to be useful, durable, and beautiful in the words of Paul Valéry. This is not by any means to say that Viguier's architecture ignores or sets aside what Valéry calls the "soul's need for beauty." There is a rigor, indeed a kind of perfection in his work that often satisfies the less material longings of visitors and users. Conviviality and contact between users of a building, or its durability are probably qualities that are not high on the list of requirements that more "artistic" architects like Gehry impose on themselves. Though Frank Gehry's Guggenheim-Bilbao has

A succession of spiral staircases and small bridges leading to the "villas" at the Avenue Jean-Jaurès.

Public Housing, Avenue Jean-Jaurès, Paris, France, 1991–94 Set near the Villette Park on the avenue Jean-Jaurès was built partially as low-cost public housing (thirty-seven units), with a further forty-seven apartments and eight artists' studios completing the structure. Set between a Renault garage and early housing built by F. Pouillon, the design seeks out transparency and lightness and converts free spaces into garden areas. As is frequently the case in the work of Jean-Paul Viguier, these elements are carefully thought out within the rigorous constraints of the public housing code. On the side of the Avenue, where it was necessary to reiterate the alignments of existing buildings, sliding glass panels with a silk-screened pattern are intended to "animate" the loggias. The budget for the complex was a relatively low eighty million Francs (1991 value).

drawn hundreds of thousands of visitors to an otherwise dull industrial city, many of its spaces are ill-suited to its main function, that of the display of art. It may be in such a case, however, that the architect was fulfilling unstated programmatic requirements of the client (i.e. drawing in the crowds) while expressing his own artistic proclivities.

Jean-Paul Viguier admits that there are certain building types he would like to experiment with — for example law courts — an area where the French government has recently called on numerous well-known architects like Portzamparc, Nouvel and Richard Rogers, but he has not succeeded in winning the competitions that he entered, such as that for the Melun courts in 1995. Just as others made their reputations building private houses or museums (like Frank Gehry), Jean-Paul Viguier is best known for his office buildings. He is chosen for his respect for the client, for the quality of construction, and for his innovative, convivial approach. These are not circumstances in which it would be appropriate to "make a ball out of a sheet of paper and pour plaster over it." Rigor and mastery of the art of architecture are what the clients want, and that is very much what Jean-Paul Viguier delivers, and at a much higher level than most of his colleagues.

Jean-Paul Viguier has spoken in terms of what he calls a "rejection of the heavy-handed, or of the pastiche," or his desire to place architecture decidedly in the movement of "progress" and "modernity." When asked how he attempts to achieve this result, he explains that it is by "drawing on materials to the point of rupture," or alternatively on the ideas behind the architecture that must be made clear "by a simple look, without so much as a drawing to explain." He emphasizes that his interest in the *lisse* (smoothness) or in emptiness, as exemplified, for example, in his atriums is not to be construed in any sense as a doctrinaire approach to architecture. Rather, these are attitudes that in the final analysis leave a mark, or constitute a style. Jean-Paul Viguier believes that the architect must play a role in the social cohesion of his environment, rather than imagining that a building in and of itself will be "socially responsible". And finally, he believes that the architect, unlike the artist, must live within a set of limits, imposed by the needs for durability or respect of the client. The architect's duty, he concludes, is to push those limits outward without transgressing them. When asked to cite an historical event of particular interest to him, Jean-Paul Viguier recalls his own experience of being in Berlin a few days before the Wall fell, a moment when "everything became possible." A breaking down of barriers, an ultimate transgression of established political order, such are the qualities that Jean-Paul Viguier admires where a history-shaping event is concerned.

Opposite page, The glass panels covering the atrium of the Cœur Défense building.

Projects

André Citroën Park   Paris, France, 1986 – 92/2000

Parisians greeted the André Citroën Park as a welcome addition to the city's green spaces. In many ways, it was, with the Villette and Bercy parks, the first to be conceived in a truly modern style. Covering thirteen hectares, it is the second largest park created in Paris since the time of Napoleon III (after the Villette). Set on a site occupied until 1972 by the Citroën automobile factories, it borders the Seine near the western limits of the city. Neighboring buildings include Richard Meier's Canal Plus Headquarters and the Georges Pompidou Hospital. An international competition organized in 1985 resulted in the rather unexpected selection of two winning teams — Jean-Paul Viguier and the landscape architect Alain Provost; and the architect Patrick Berger working with Gilles Clément. A collaboration, with each participant contributing more extensively to given areas of the park came about as a result of this duality of the competition selection. The basic design of the park, is dependent on a central void, a rectangular field measuring 320 × 130 meters, running perpendicular to the Seine. At the far end of this lawn, two forty-five meter long greenhouses designed by Patrick Berger emphasize the axial arrangement of the space, also highlighted by a "grand canal" conceived by Viguier bordered by seven small stone pavilions. Jean-Paul Viguier was called on to extend and complete the original park scheme with a one hundred-twenty meter viaduct placed perpendicularly to the main garden rectangle, not far from the banks of the Seine. The goal of this bridge, which carries train traffic, was to permit visitors to the park to go freely up to the river. This is in fact the only place in Paris where it is possible to walk from the city to the riverbank without having to cross any roads. The elegant white arc of the viaduct now serves as a visible sign of the André Citroën Park from the river itself or from the Right Bank. With his more recent France Télévision Headquarters, Jean-Paul Viguier has thus created two significant elements of the urban design of western Paris on the Left Bank.

Previous double-page:
A general view of the
park, with the green-
houses by Patrick Berger
visible on the right.

This page:
The relative simplicity of
the central part of the
garden is underlined by
Viguier's strong canal
with its regularly spaced
stone structure. Above
right on this image,
Richard Meier's Canal +
Headquarters Building.

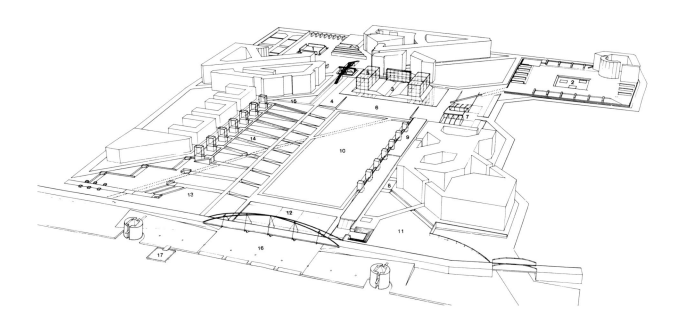

Despite the rigorous axiality of the Park, with the canal leading down towards the Seine (above left), it provides a convivial and open space that Parisians greatly appreciate.

French Pavilion, Expo '92 Seville, Spain, 1989 – 92

Set in the grounds of the 1992 Universal Exhibition in Seville, the French Pavilion was one of the most radical buildings ever designed in such circumstances. At the heart of the space, where many architects would have deployed their most dazzling effects, Jean-Paul Viguier chose to create a spectacular void. An open, one thousand square meter esplanade, raised one and a half meters above grade covered a space called the "Image Well." Twenty-five meters long, twenty-one wide and seventeen meters deep, this well was designed to contain a five hundred square meter IMAX screen. Above ground, a narrow exhibition structure, called the mirror building, was set back from the esplanade and the whole was covered by a fifty by fifty-five meter "sky" suspended fifteen meters above the glass slab surface. This five hundred-ton structure was designed so that its four hollow stainless steel support columns and the blue polyester clad sky they supported would be almost invisible. This series of figures underlines the structural reality of a pavilion characterized more by its absence than by its presence. Undeniably modern in its appearance, the design was nonetheless quite different from almost any other notable modern building. Rather than digging into the earth, most "modernist" buildings tend to appear to sit lightly on the ground without fundamentally disturbing its surface. Here, the open sky of Seville and its excavated soil formed mirror-image voids, above and below grade. The transparency and fluidity of this design, which successfully handled millions of visitors, are indicative of several related characteristics of Jean-Paul Viguier's work: his fascination with complex yet almost invisible technical solutions adapted to each project; his determination to make his designs "smooth" (lisse); and his fundamental modesty even when significant buildings are involved.

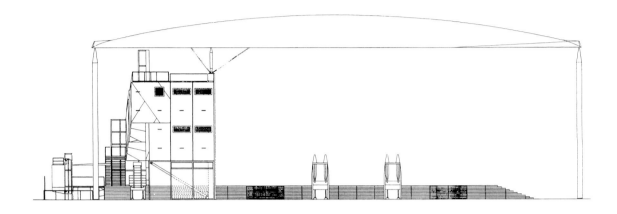

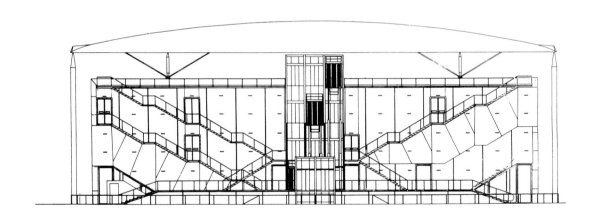

As photos and cross-sections of the Pavilion show, the immaterial impression conveyed by the structure actually provided substantial exhibition space, both below the central square (above left) and in the associated display building (below left).

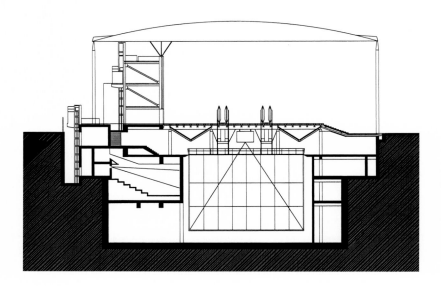

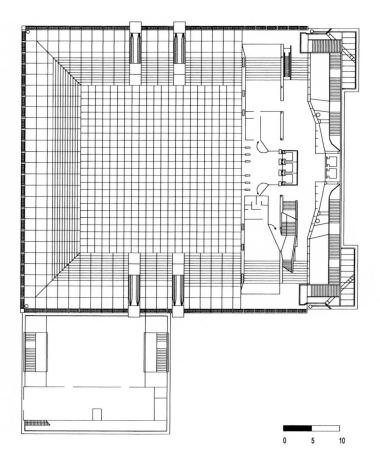

A plan of the square
and a cross-section
show that the open
platform of the Pavilion
(above and above
right) was in fact the
roof of a large under-
ground projection
area. The linear dis-
plays in the annex
building provided a
more traditional pavil-
ion area (below right).

0   5   10

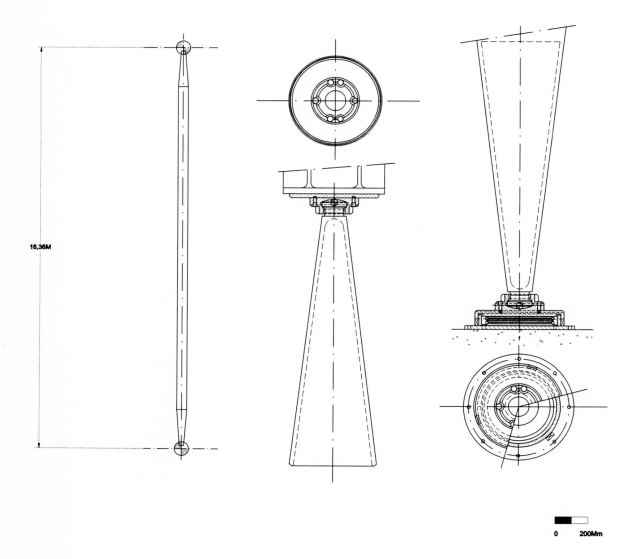

16,36M

0   200Mm

One of the aspects of
the Pavilion that Jean-
Paul Viguier is most
proud of is the sophis-
ticated columns that
he designed to hold
up the "sky" or roof
above the central plat-
form of the structure.

Pont du Gard, Visitor Center, Museum and Site Renovation   Nîmes, France, 1992 – 2001

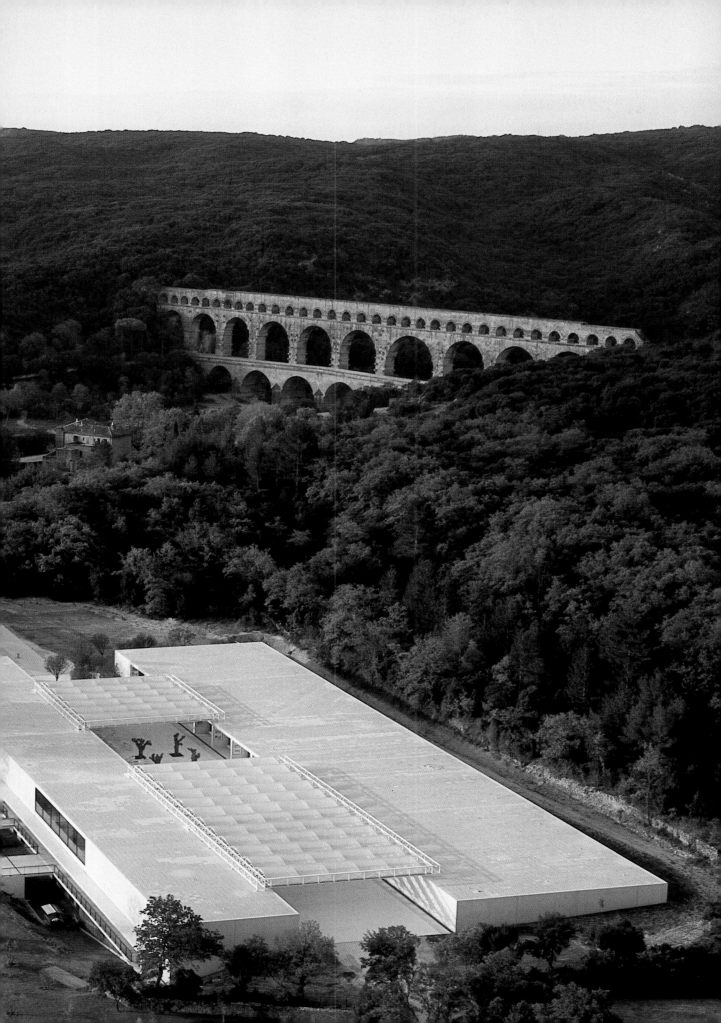

The historic Roman aqueduct called the Pont du Gard is visited by up to ten thousand persons per day in the summer. Until it was decided to renovate its site, the monument was in the midst of a jumble of poorly conceived tourism-related structures. Jean-Paul Viguier chose to clear the area immediately around the bridge, allowing visitors to discover it suddenly as they walk along a two hundred-meter approach path. The complexity of the program was heightened not only by the sensitivity of the site, but also by the need to house numerous functions, including relocated boutiques in a dignified, efficient group of volumes. A three hundred seat auditorium; permanent exhibition space on the history of the aqueduct; a teaching area for children up to fourteen years of age; a temporary exhibition area; a center for documentation on this site and other similar ones; and administrative offices form the cultural core of the design. An eight hundred-car parking lot is set in adjacent agricultural fields, invisible from the monument. The actual buildings, made of concrete colored like local stone, are discrete, as the museum demonstrates. This two thousand six hundred square meter volume is inserted into the natural site, descending as much as 6.6 meters below grade. A central, rectangular space (115 × 18 meters) with a ceiling height of eight meters is intended to offer a spectacular, flexible exhibition area. The architect was also involved in the landscape architecture of the site and in the choice of the American artist James Turrell to provide a new lighting system for the aqueduct. The whole is integrated into a smoothly conceived system that leads visitors from their cars or buses to the ticketing or museum and shop areas and on to the object of their visit. Here as in other projects, Jean-Paul Viguier demonstrates his ability to resolve complex architectural and site-related problems with a subtlety and efficiency that corresponds directly to his personality.

← Pont du Gard

↑

Previous double-page:
An aerial view shows
the new buildings
designed by Viguier and
the landscaping leading
up to the Pont du Gard
(visible at the upper
right).

This page:
An approach path
designed by Jean-Paul
Viguier, with the Pont
du Gard visible in the
background.

The low-rise configuration of the facility permits it to blend into the surroundings, without giving up its modernist identity. The architect goes so far as to use the natural rock of the site (left).

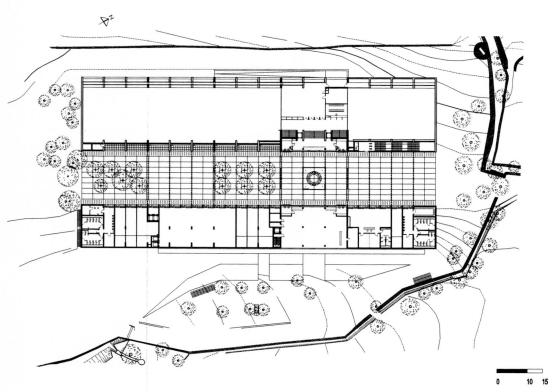

Plans of the museum
(left) and visitor
center (below) and
a general view of the
visitor center (above).

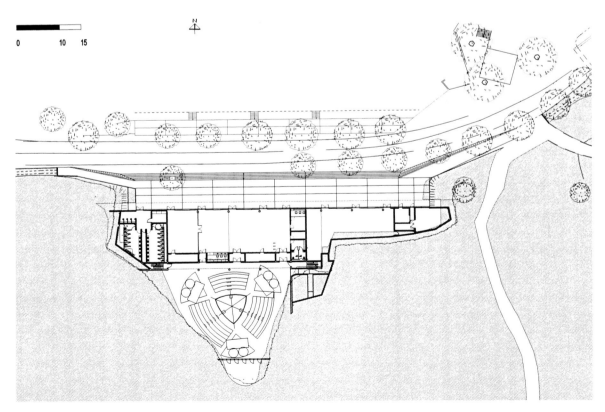

0   10   15

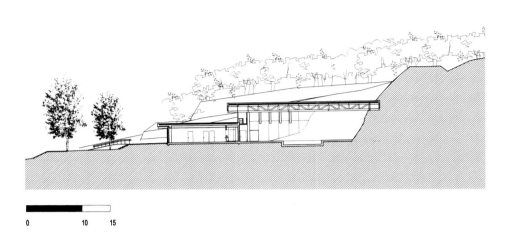

0   10   15

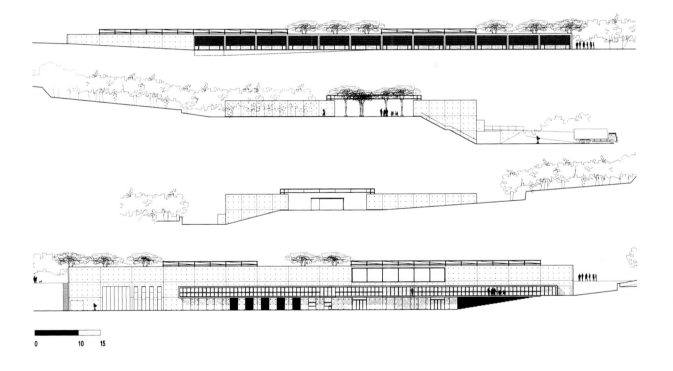

0   10   15

The visitor center is set into the rocks of a relatively modern quarry (cross-section above).

Both in section and images, the longitudinal design of the visitor center demonstrates its insertion into the landscape of the site.

GEC Alsthom Transport Headquarters   Saint-Ouen, France, 1993–97

Located near Paris, this seventeen thousand square meter complex was built by Jean-Paul Viguier subsequent to his selection in a 1993 competition. The client, a major builder of railroad equipment, needed a headquarters for a staff of eight hundred persons. After having been situated in a tower in the Défense area of Paris, the firm insisted on the need for better communication among staff. Viguier's solution, which might be linked indirectly to that of the Ford Foundation in New York, was to create a semi-circular atrium whose function he compares to that of a "communications turbine." Bridges cut through the six levels of open space around a central elevator shaft. The firm's project groups are allotted sections of the circular office space that can either be connected or isolated as circumstances require. Given GEC Alsthom's insistence on communication, Viguier naturally chose conviviality as one of the leitmotifs of this structure, placing a library, cafeteria and a small museum on the ground floor near the entrance. Oak flooring contributes a feeling of warmth to the interior spaces. Despite the spectacular central atrium, an emphasis has been placed on sobriety as well, with exterior cladding laid out in simple bands of glass and metal. An elegant aluminum and steel brise soleil on the city side of the structure highlights its refinement and brings to mind the very fine columns designed for the French Pavilion at Expo '92. With this building, Jean-Paul Viguier obviously dealt first and foremost with the requirements of the client. His solution, however, calls on a broad spectrum of architectural knowledge and historical references. From Kevin Roche's Ford Foundation, reaching back to the famous "Prisons" of Piranesi, or other prison design, the GEC Alsthom Transport Headquarters is a model of transparency and modernity.

Previous double-page:
The atrium of the GEC
Alsthom Headquarters
conveys the Piranesian
feeling that is frequently
present in the architec-
ture of Jean-Paul Viguier,
this despite his rigorous
modernist stance.

This page:
A view of the entrance
bridge also gives a ver-
tiginous impression of
the architect's use of
space.

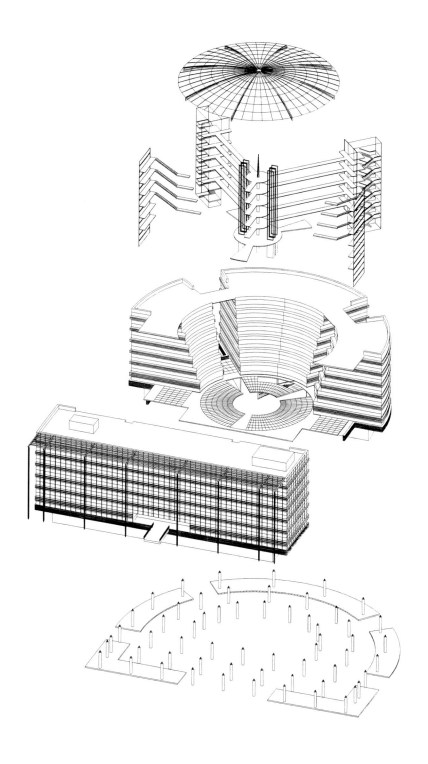

An exploded axono-
metric drawing of the
GEC building clearly
underlines the rigor of
the geometric design,
combining a rectangu-
lar volume with a
semi-circular one.
The simplicity of the
form is clearly visible
in the aerial view to
the left.

61

The multiple bridges crossing the void at the heart of the building are reminiscent not only of the architecture of Kevin Roche, but also of that of Richard Meier. Again, the imagery of Piranesi is brought to mind.

Congress Center Auditorium   Marseille, France, 1994 – 97

Built following a competition in 1994, this extension to an existing conference facility is located in the Chanot Park where the city of Marseille holds its industrial exhibitions. The three thousand five hundred meter surface of the structure is given over essentially to a twelve hundred-seat auditorium destined to conferences, movies and concerts. An entrance foyer and technical facilities make up the rest of the building. The fan-shaped design opens out onto the park and is connected to the existing building via a covered transparent bridge. Despite its apparently unusual configuration, the building fits into the existing orthogonal system of the park, giving both the original Congress Center and the space itself a coherence that it lacked until the intervention of Jean-Paul Viguier. Two large concrete walls mark the outer limits of the building, with a large glass opening along the entire curved façade providing ample daylight for the triple-height foyer. Both the foyer and the auditorium itself are clad in wood. Here as in other buildings, Viguier compensates for the somewhat "hard" aspect of some of his materials with daylight and warmer materials such as wood.

An interior view of the 1200 seat auditorium (previous double-page) contrasts with the transparent articulation of the entrance (this page). Viguier's strict sense of volume and materials is apparent in this image.

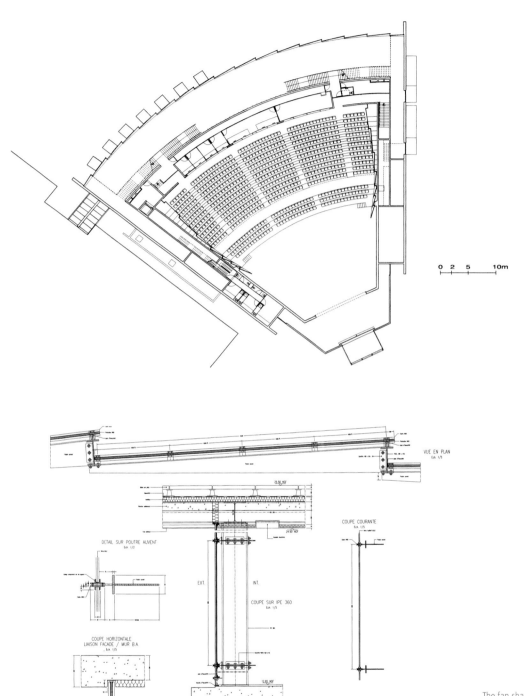

The fan shape of the auditorium is apparent both in the floor plan above and in the sweeping curves visible from the exterior of the building. To the left, drawings of the canopy structure.

Opposite page:
The play on horizontal, vertical and diagonal lines, together with a careful orchestration of materials make for a composition that is typical of the architect's work.

This page:
The stairway leading up to the main entrances of the auditorium.

Public Housing, ZAC Bercy   Paris, France, 1994 – 98

This four thousand eight hundred square meter public housing project was built following a 1994 competition for a budget of thirty-one million French Francs. The fifty-two apartments are situated in an eight-story structure located on the corner of the rue Baron Leroy, the rue de l'Aubrac, and the rue François Truffaut. The disposition of the plan generates an easily accessible internal courtyard garden. A four hundred twenty square meter area on the street side was earmarked for shops while duplex apartments are arrayed on the garden side. The façade is made up of two layers: an inner layer clad in white stone in which generous glazed openings are set, and an outer layer with railings in white stone and metal with moveable glass panels intended to provide an agreeable "loggia" for each apartment. Alternating the bands of stone and the windows in an irregular pattern, Jean-Paul Viguier succeeds in animating what is otherwise a geometrically regulated scheme. This is indeed a recurring characteristic in his work: a concern for geometric regularity and "smoothness" blended with an artistic sense for movement and variety especially in elements related to the cladding. With a total of eight stories (including the ground floor), the building has an upper level that provides three duplexes and three studios with planted terrasses. Part of an urban development scheme (ZAC Bercy) this apartment building is located near the Bercy Park, and just across the river from the French National Library.

Previous double-page and this page: The façades of the building offer a rich composition of opaque and transparent elements. The firm lines of each story give a rhythm to the composition, allowing for variations in the sliding window patterns without sacrificing the overall harmony of the architecture.

There is an almost industrial hardness to some of Viguier's compositions, here on a terrace of the building, and yet the almost musical variety he introduces into his own rigidity softens his work and reveals some of its interest (right).

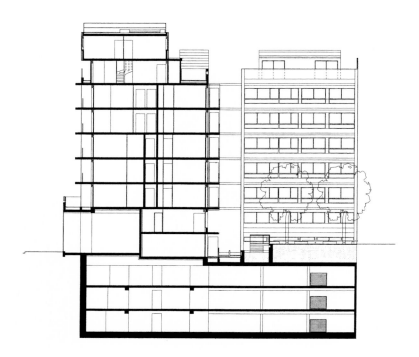

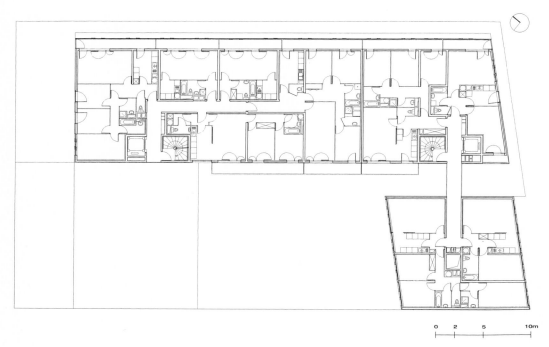

0 2 5 10m

This page:
Plan and section show
that the apparent
strictness of the
composition allows for
variations such as the
angled walls visible in
the floor plan of the
housing above.

Opposite page:
The kind of atrium
effect seen on a much
larger scale in the
France Télévision
Building is here
adapted to a
residential format.

Astra France Headquarters   Rueil-Malmaison, France, 1994 – 97

Built as the headquarters of the pharmaceutical company Astra, this ten thousand square meter building provides for a possible five thousand meter future extension. The design is made up from two volumes, a long rectangular block and a stepped, angled block opposite, the two sections being joined at the center by a generous atrium. Winner of the 1999 Business Week/Architectural Record Award, the Astra Headquarters was cited by jury member William Pederson in the following terms: "The architect paid meticulous attention to detail, it's a very comfortable environment — where nature plays an important role — one that seems more human than almost any of the corporate headquarters we saw." Set just outside of Paris, the building contains two hundred forty offices each measuring thirteen square meters (directors get double this figure). Swedish natural wood furniture and an extensive use of wood elsewhere in the building have led a number of commentators to say that the Astra Headquarters has a decidedly "Nordic" feeling to it. Given that Astra is a Swedish based company, this reference is entirely appropriate. An extensive use of bridges and walkways animates the interior space and makes movement between the offices easy. Playing both on the interior courtyard and on windows facing the exterior, Viguier gives an exceptional openness to the otherwise identical offices. Both within and without, he makes use of a cladding system that emphasizes alternating bands — of metal and glass, or metal and wood. Horizontality and verticality are frequently contrasted, thus avoiding any danger of a static appearance. Built for a budget of ten thousand (1994) French Francs per square meter, the Astra Headquarters is cited too as a model of ergonomic comfort. Details ranging from air flow to the size of the parking spots were thought out in meticulous detail by the architect to give the whole a conviviality and a feeling of durability that were certainly high on the client's list of priorities.

This page:
Glass, steel and stone
give the Astra Building
a "Nordic" aspect that
clearly appealed to the
client.

Here opacity and transparency are contrasted on a large scale, allowing light into the heart of the building. The horizontal banding of the closed surfaces is also contrasted with the vertical thrust of the glazed areas.

Wood and stone give
a feeling of solidity
to the building. The
wood cladding also
serves to offset the
harder materials and
the strict geometric
alignments.

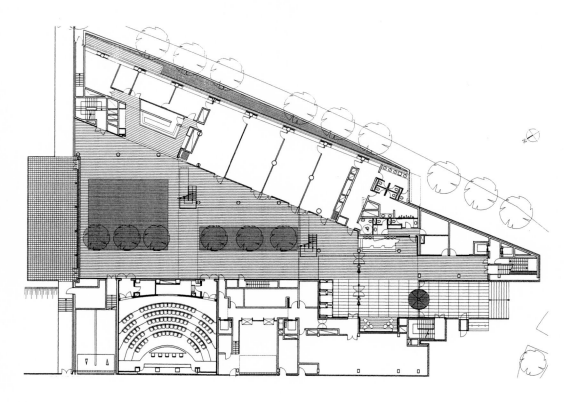

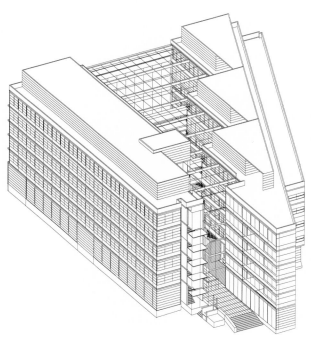

In a floor plan and an axonometric view, the role of the atrium is made clear. Banks of stairways highlight the architect's taste for repetitive patterns.

France Télévision Headquarters   Paris, France, 1994–98

This fifty-six thousand square meter building houses the offices of the two French government television stations, France 2 and France 3. The two thousand five hundred employees of the networks are housed in a triangular plan structure articulated around internal courtyards and a spectacular entrance atrium. A one hundred twenty-meter façade signals the presence of the building on the Left Bank of the Seine, at the eastern extremity of Paris, not far from the André Citroën Park and Richard Meier's Canal Plus building. Situated where it is, France Télévision Headquarters can be assimilated to the eastern gate of the city. Despite the large mass of the structure, Jean-Paul Viguier has successfully used an almost painterly façade design to enliven the volumes. While fully respecting his own principle of smoothness (lisse) in the cladding, he alternates bands of clear, and sandblasted glass with strips of white Thracian marble, in an abstract pattern easily perceived from the neighboring roads. Technically, and in terms of its resolution of programmatic complexities, the France Télévision Headquarters is a masterful, modern office complex. Since France 2 is a much larger organization than France 3, the architect was led to create separate but unequal office areas for each firm, while giving the impression that one group does not dominate the other. The architect's technical prowess is demonstrated in the successful construction of the television studios in the building's lower level, near to a high-speed commuter train line. Vibration and noise are all but eliminated through a complex system of dampers devised by Jean-Paul Viguier. Despite its scale and regular plan, the building offers a surprising number of unusual spaces, such as the topmost level, just beneath the entrance atrium skylights. Here the sophisticated, smooth finishing of the offices gives way to a Piranesian roughness, a dizzying twenty-five meters above the atrium floor. Looking outwards, the building, which is high by Paris standards, offers spectacular views onto the Seine and the rest of the city.

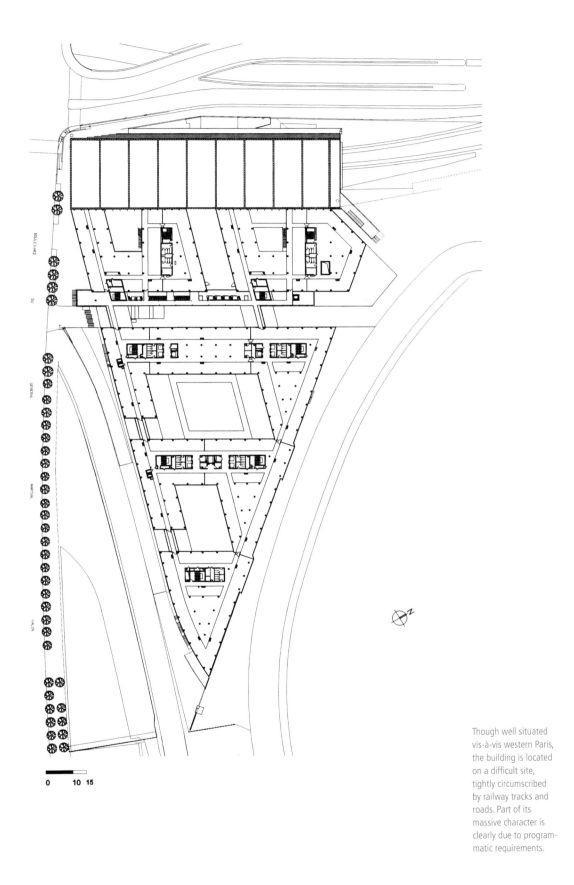

0   10 15

Though well situated
vis-à-vis western Paris,
the building is located
on a difficult site,
tightly circumscribed
by railway tracks and
roads. Part of its
massive character is
clearly due to program-
matic requirements.

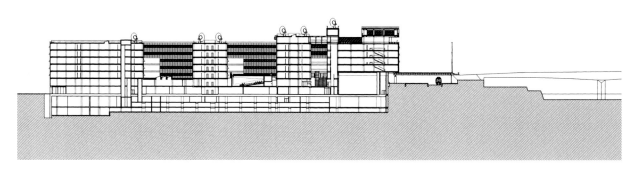

0   10 15

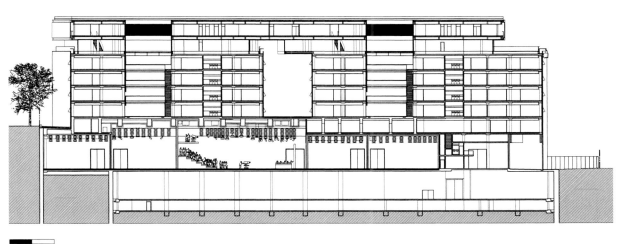

0   5   10

Set deeply into the embankments of the Seine, the France Télévision Headquarters has recording studios located partially below grade.

The urban complexity of the site is visible in the Seine-side view above left. Below left, the long, horizontal bar that extends inland from the Seine (located to the left on this image) is accentuated by the banded cladding.

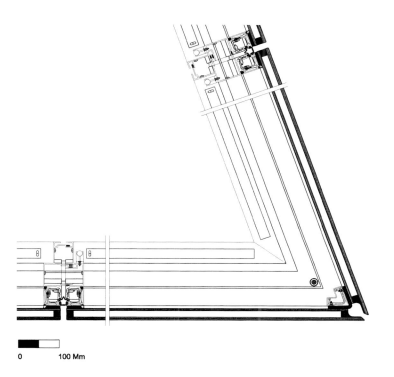

0   100 Mm

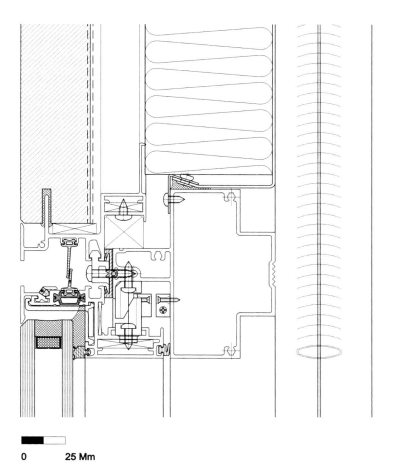

0   25 Mm

Viguier's drawings, showing the glass assembly at an edge of the building (above) and the complexity of the system required to obtain the *lisse* he seeks in the cladding (below), show the hidden aspects that result in the smoothness of the façade to the left.

This large shopping center project includes space for a seventeen theater multiplex cinema, sports areas, restaurants, gas stations and five thousand parking spots, as well as the more traditional supermarkets and boutiques. Measuring a total of over one hundred thousand square meters, the shopping center, originally baptized Francilia, includes some forty-five thousand square meters of retail space. It is set in the so-called Servigny ZAC, a development area located near the center of the future town of Sénart. The basic scheme is laid out within the limits of a three hundred sixty-five meter square. The actual shopping center is set on two levels each six meters high, designed in a triangular form. The roof extends above the entrance area, with a generous fifteen-meter high canopy. This canopied entrance in fact corresponds to the city-side of the project, while the parking areas, arranged on the opposite side, are hidden from view. The architect emphasizes the exceptional character of this gesture toward the new city, whereas most shopping centers give little if any care to their openness, preferring a more economically driven "shoe-box" mentality. Within, a system based on two large, curved walkways with natural lighting guides visitors to the different stores. A light color scheme, together with this abundance of lighting and frequent views toward the city will give the whole a conviviality for which the architect is known. Façade detailing, near the entrance canopy for example, follows the usual pattern established by Viguier in his other work, with large horizontal bands, corresponding to the windows where there is glazing and to intermediary space where stone or metal cladding intervenes. The architect believes firmly that glazing is only to be used where there are actually windows, and not simply to cover the intermediary spaces between each floor. The horizontality of the façade is off set by the elegant columns supporting the canopy.

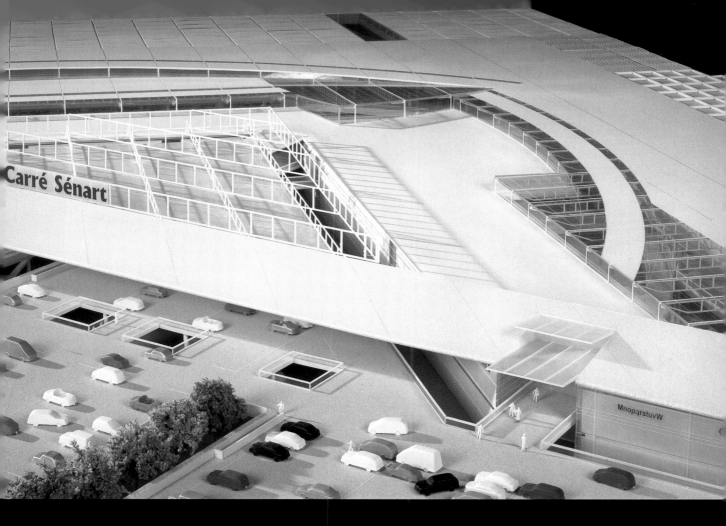

Carré Sénart

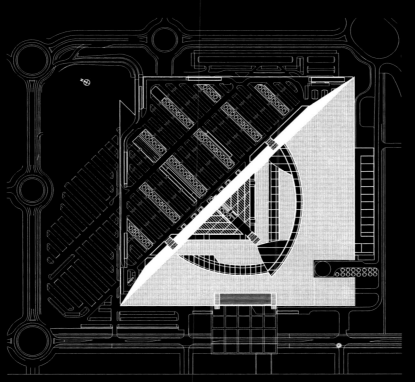

MnopqrstuvW

0   20   40

Previous double-page and this page: Plans and models for the Carré Sénart Shopping Center clearly demonstrate how the architect divides a basic geometric space (the square or *carré*) to obtain the requisite parking areas (upper left on the plan on this page) and animates it with circular elements and a triangular design.

For the Media Center, Jean-Paul Viguier faced a complex problem, namely the proximity of a world-renowned historic monument, the Reims Cathedral. It can be said that Richard Meier in Ulm or Norman Foster in Nîmes were confronted with similar problems. Like Meier and Foster before him, Jean-Paul Viguier opted for the only language he knows in architecture, that of modernity, but a modernity that is respectful of its environment. The sixty million French Franc building does have one rather unexpected aspect, it conserves the façade of the late 19th century Police Headquarters, while removing the roof of the older building, and setting the whole complex at a uniform fifteen meter height. This gesture immediately gives the impression that the two volumes form a whole, and a rather classical one, opposite the Gothic extravagance of the Cathedral. The architect points out that demolishing the Police Head-quarters would have only aggravated the impression that very little is left of pre-War Reims. "The city had already suffered enough," he says, a position for which he has been amply criticized. The black metal and glass façade is intended to be a distant reminder of the spine-like structure of the Cathedral, while a base made of Courville stone is a bow to the tradition of local masonry. From within, glass roofing over the corner closest to the church permits visitors to admire the full height of the older structure. Although Viguier's problem here was quite different from that of Foster in Nîmes opposite the Roman Maison Carré, both architects opted for a classical simplicity, which neither denies their own modern roots nor struggles uselessly for attention opposite a great monument. Despite Viguier's respectful attitude, local authorities took the unusual step of asking the French Minister of Culture (at the time Catherine Trautmann) to give the final go-ahead for the project, due to considerable opposition from their own constituencies.

Previous double-page:
This façade drawing of the Center shows the reflection of the Reims Cathedral, located opposite.

This page:
With a typical play on materials and the use of alternating vertical and horizontal bands, Viguier gives a richness and animation to the façade.

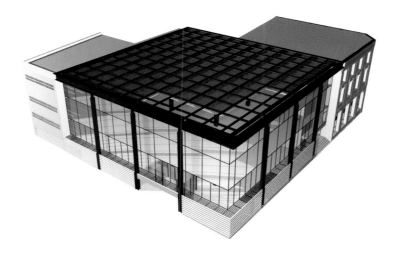

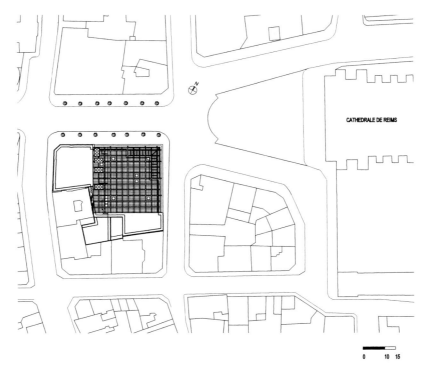

CATHEDRALE DE REIMS

0   10 15

Opposite page:
Construction views
showing the location
of the site vis-à-vis
the Cathedral, and
the façades of the old
police building.

Above:
An axonometric of the
building as seen from
the Cathedral — the
old police building is
to the right.

Tong Ji University Franco-Chinese Center   Shanghai, China, 1997 –

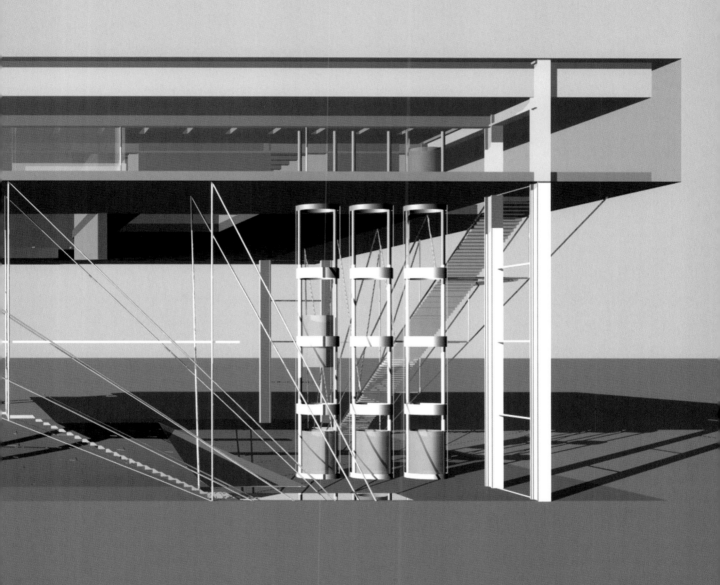

With colleagues like Jean-Marie Charpentier (Shanghai Opera) and Paul Andreu (Shanghai Pudong Airport, Beijing Opera) leading the way, French architects have earned considerable attention in China recently. Jean-Paul Viguier's presence in China is related to an agreement signed between the French engineering school Ponts et Chaussées and the University of Tong Ji. This agreement is based on research, teaching and assistance to corporations, but included the decision to build a Franco-Chinese Center on the campus of the University, in Shanghai. Jean-Paul Viguier emphasizes that his design, although decidedly modern in appearance, makes clear reference to Chinese thought. Formed from a square divided into nine parts, the basic structure emerges with the removal of the ninth part to obtain the number eight, that the Chinese consider to have beneficial qualities. The ninth element remains as a freestanding fifty-meter circular tower for office space. This freestanding tower also curiously brings to mind the campanile tradition of Italy. The main building is divided in two sections, with the entrance and exhibition area below grade, and the teaching and amphitheater area suspended above. The gap between the suspended part of the structure and its underground counterpart is also the result of a study of Feng Shui, considered essential to building design in China. Viguier has strongly implicated himself in this project, accepting an occasional professorial role and working with Tong Ji professors and students on his own project for the Franco-Chinese Center. "French architects are strongly attracted to Asia, and particularly to Chinese culture," he says. "They like this situation where tradition and modernity have to live together, maybe because in France it is the current state of the art."

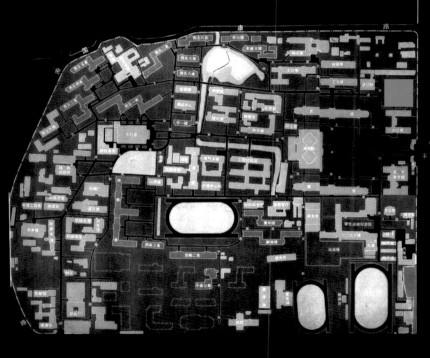

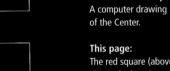 

Previous double-page:
A computer drawing
of the Center.

This page:
The red square (above)
shows the location
of the Center in the
campus. To the left,
drawings showing
the vertical circulation
in the building.

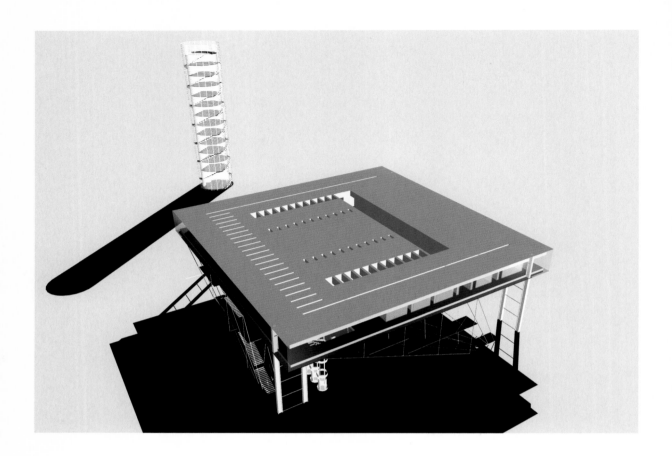

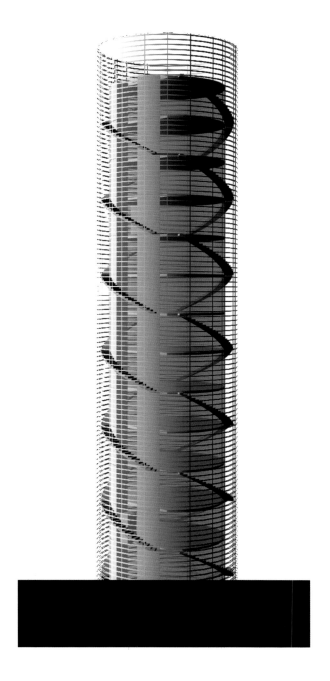

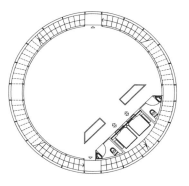

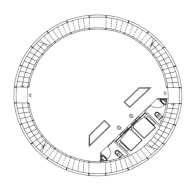

Computer drawings of the Center with the circular tower (on this page) visible to the upper left of the main structure (opposite page, top).

The suspended volume and square plan recall the French Pavilion in Seville, while the round tower may, for some bring to mind the work of Toyo Ito.

Cœur Défense Office Building   Paris, France, 1997 – 2001

This is one of Jean-Paul Viguier's most visible and important projects in the French capital. The three hundred fifty thousand square meter complex is set not far from the historic Parisian axis, leading from the Louvre to the Arch of the Défense. It is made up of twin towers, each one hundred eighty meters tall, and three lower buildings, each of eight stories. The entire complex is linked by an atrium that soars to a height of forty-four meters and covers one hectare in area. It is clear that on this site of the former Esso Tower, Jean-Paul Viguier wanted to differentiate his project from that of surrounding towers. The Défense is one of the very few areas of Paris where modern architecture dominates and tall buildings are permitted. Rather than opting for what he calls the "thick" tower typology, the architect chose to design fine silhouettes, only twenty-three meters wide and eighty meters long. Together with their rounded ends, this makes for a refinement that permits the Cœur Défense to indeed look unlike anything in its environment while still fitting well into the neighborhood. Within the tower each office floor is outfitted in similar manner in order to be as flexible as possible. Although contingencies of use dictate most of his decisions, he has found an innovative way to make these towers appear to change as the day progresses. A sixteen-centimeter gap filled with pressurized air between the double-glazing permits the use of mechanical shades that can be controlled manually but also open and close according to the building's exposure to the sun. The result is that when all the shades are closed, the towers take on a uniform horizontal banding familiar to Viguier. When they open, they do so in irregular patterns that animate the façade in different ways each day. Working carefully on details and engineering as he always does, Viguier has created a massive atrium space that fits well into this admittedly very large complex. As in so many other projects, he has underlined conviviality and communication, through the means of the atrium.

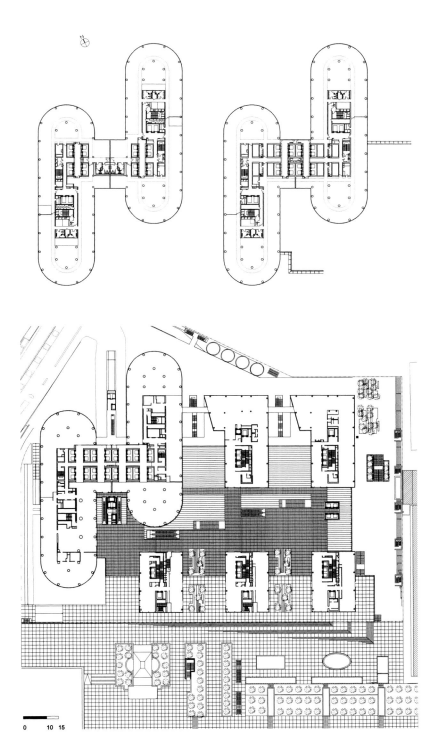

0   10 15

A photo on the left and plans on this page, show the staggered location of the twin towers.

The overall floor plan shows how the towers are integrated into the whole, with the dark area representing the vast atrium.

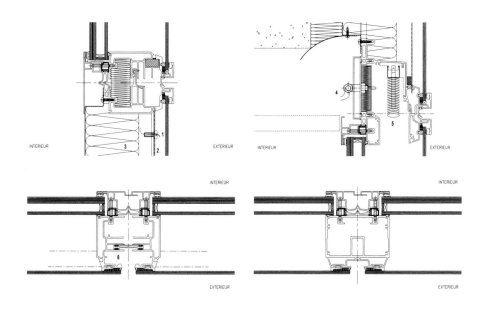

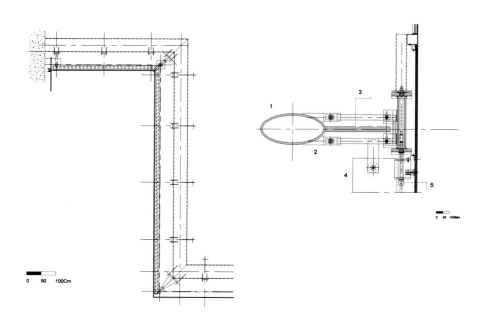

This page:
Drawings showing
the design of the
double pressurized
air windows and the
angles of the structure.

**Opposite page and
following double-
page:** The atrium.

Sofitel Hotel Chicago, Illinois, United States, 1998–2002

Building in Chicago in a central location, in this case near Michigan Avenue on Wabash, is a challenge for any architect, and perhaps especially for one who is inspired by modern masters such as Mies van der Rohe, whose Lake Shore Drive apartments are not far away. Jean-Paul Viguier was all the more honored to receive this commission because he beat two local stars, Helmut Jahn and Julien La Grange in the competition. This thirty-five thousand square meter building was intended by the French Accor hotel group to give a new image to its Sofitel chain. The hotel includes four hundred fifteen rooms on thirty-tree floors, with three floors for public space and receptions. Jean-Paul Viguier's description of the building calls for resolving three major needs: first a generous opening of the public spaces of the hotel out onto those of the city; second a composition of the volumes that takes into account the horizontal orientation of the public spaces and the vertical stacking of the hotel rooms; and third an audacious architecture intended to create an emblematic presence in the city. A monumental staircase connects the visible public spaces to the private ones. True to his usual position, Viguier alternates glass and white stone bands on the exterior, highlighting a horizontality that has a dynamic interaction with the fundamental verticality of the tower. The use of a light-colored stone also differentiates the tower from its mostly darker environment that includes the enormous John Hancock Tower. The emblematic presence of the hotel is assured more than anything else by the forward thrusting "prow" of the structure, angled out towards the street and narrowing as it rises. The angularity of the tower permits many of the guest rooms to have spectacular views onto the city. With its fundamental geometric simplicity and its attention to detailing, this first major building for Jean-Paul Viguier in Chicago is an appropriate homage to the city that gave birth to the modern tower.

PARK

Public
Self
Park
←

CERTI
SAVER

Previous double page:
The Sofitel stands out
with its white, angular
volume in this aerial
view of Chicago.

This page:
A construction photo
shows the protruding
angle of the hotel with
the massive John
Hancock Tower in the
background.

Right:
Volumetric drawings
showing the way in
which the form of the
structure was
generated.

Below:
A ground floor plan
and a typical upper
floor plan.

Opposite page:
The entrance area
echoes the dynamic
angle of the tower
itself, curving outward
and up.

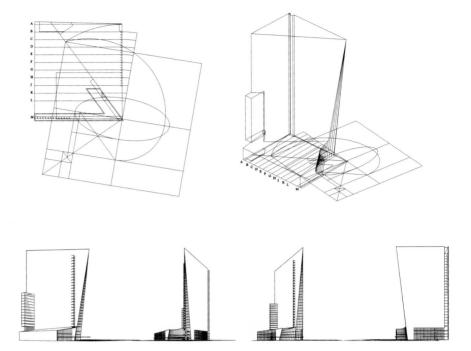

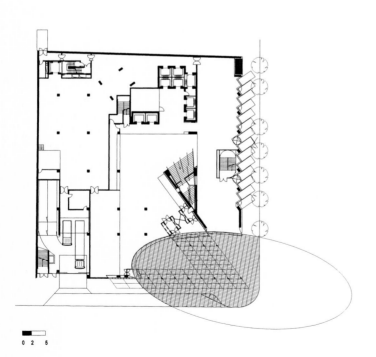

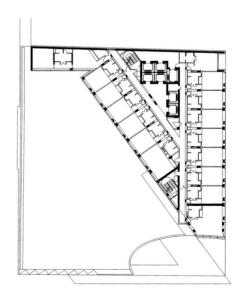

0 2 5

Bristol Myers Squibb Headquarters   Rueil-Malmaison, France, 1999 – 2002

This is a twenty thousand meter corporate headquarters for a pharmaceutical company, located like Astra in Rueil-Malmaison near Paris. It is intended for a staff of eight hundred persons and can be expanded in a second phase to accommodate four hundred fifty more in a ten thousand square meter extension. A two thousand meter outdoor courtyard is already planned as part of the complex, linking the first and second phases. Both the corporate restaurant and the meeting rooms have a direct access to this garden. Clearly expressing Jean-Paul Viguier's interest in geometric plans, the structure is laid out along a one hundred and fifty meter curve forming a section of a circle. A cladding in alternating horizontal bands, a sort of Viguier trademark, highlights the dynamic movement inferred by the curvature of the eight-story structure. A system of modular meeting rooms is integrated into the plan on the second floor. At once conservative and dynamic in its appearance, this headquarters offers ample evidence as to why large corporate clients have called frequently on Jean-Paul Viguier. He has shown an obvious capacity to respect the programmatic requirements of the clients while creating an agreeable and modern working place. Ease of circulation, proximity to sources of daylight and to the natural environment wherever possible, together with a fluid capacity to integrate essentially repetitive office elements into a varied and coherent whole—all of these factors are essential to the efficiency and well-being of any corporate staff. The point is clearly not for the architect to make a personal statement, although by the repetition of certain gestures, he does create a recognizable style—a style that he adopts with great dexterity to varying circumstances.

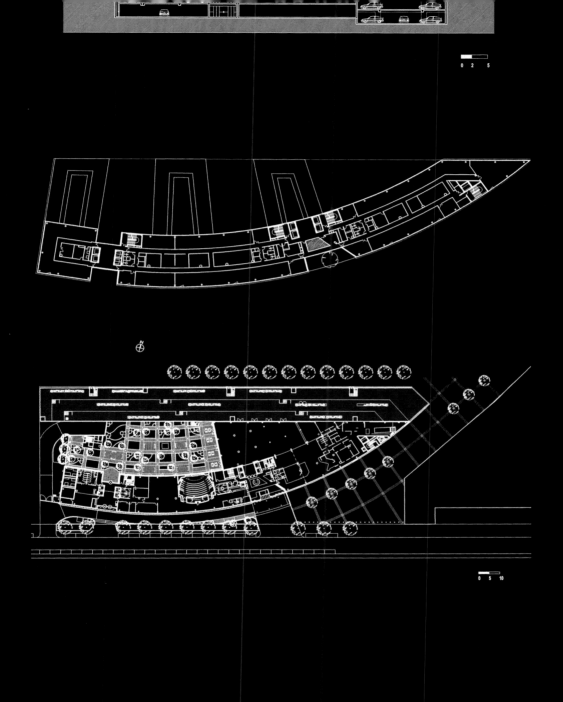

0 2 5

0 5 10

This project combines the rehabilitation of an existing structure (two thousand five hundred square meters) and the construction of a new building (three thousand three hundred square meters) directly connected to the old museum. Jean-Paul Viguier has also been given the responsibility of the museum layout and of a botanical garden. Working with Alain Provost, who also collaborated on the André Citroën Park, Viguier's mission is to create a new unified entity out of the three parts of the project. Exhibition areas in the form of two large un-encumbered floors are grouped in the new building, while the organization of activities and information are concentrated in the old building. A large curved glass façade is intended as the architectural linking element between the old, the new, and the botanical garden. The sober, horizontal design of this new part of the museum is intended to allow the old building and the neighboring church continue to play their roles in the urban environment. Insofar as the museum design is concerned, Viguier wants to clearly separate actual objects of historic value from those conceived as part of evocations of natural history. He also feels it is important to "tease" the visitor by not giving away the whole scheme too quickly, thus inciting the visitor to go to the end of the visit. Like the museum itself, which makes use of an existing structure, the garden too is designed around specimens planted earlier. The resulting three hundred sixty-five meter long "spiral" is intended as a journey of initiation accompanied by a small stream. Both within and without, the idea entertaining and drawing visitors forward is present in the project descriptions as much as actual architectural details. This is indicative of Jean-Paul Viguier's respect for the function of his architecture, and his laudable tendency to put clients in the forefront of his preoccupations.

With a renovated garden echoing the arc of the inner façade of the new building, Viguier here demonstrates an obvious capacity to fit a modern design into an historical context.

Above:
The curved façade
facing out onto the
botanical garden.

Right:
The plan shows the
integration of the
ground floor design
and that of the garden.

Opposite page:
Cross sections showing
the relationship of the
new spaces to the old.

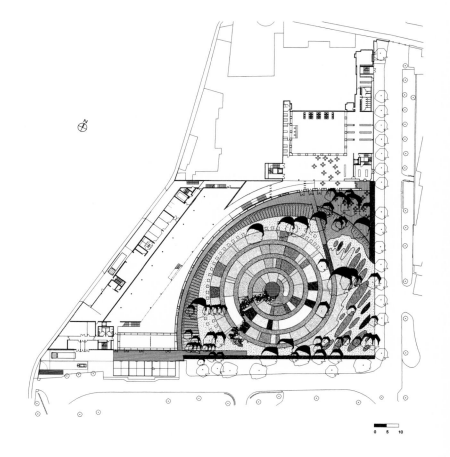

0 5 10

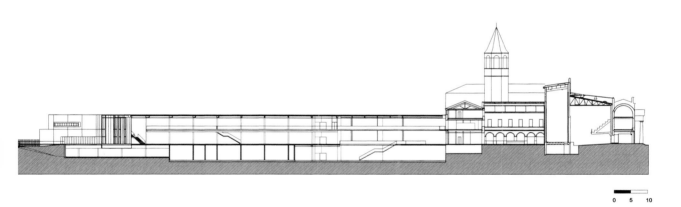

0   5   10

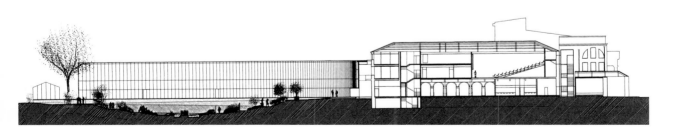

Ilôt M7 Office Building   Paris, France, 2000 – 2003

Set in the new ZAC Rive Gauche development area not far from Dominique Perrault's French National Library, this complex includes eleven thousand square meters of office space and three thousand two hundred meters of housing. It is built over railroad tracks that approach the nearby Austerlitz Station. The office space includes two five hundred seat corporate cafeterias and one hundred seventy five parking spots. Aligned on the Avenue de France, two nine story buildings both eighteen meters thick, one hundred meters long, and the other fifty-nine are placed setting the outer limits of the area, with two seven story buildings set inside this urban "island". Jean-Paul Viguier emphasizes the "domestic" or "urban" appearance of his design as opposed to the more strictly repetitive schemes often seen for this kind of large mixed-use project. Light colored stone and lacquered metal have been chosen for cladding, respecting Viguier's usual preference for a transparent glass in the windows. An irregular pattern applied to the rhythm of cladding and glazing breaks the monotony of the otherwise rigorously geometric design. The use of stone panels is regulated to control exposure to the sun. The openness of the complex is further emphasized by the creation of an eight and one half meter high gallery on the side of the Avenue de France where stores will be installed. The columns in this area are flared out towards the bottom, visualizing the transfer of the building's weight towards the ground. This gesture, although apparently insignificant is in fact an indication of the architect's constant interest in expressing the technical or engineering side of his work. It is not that the engineering is put forward to be seen, but neither is there the pretense that architecture can be achieved without any visible means of support.

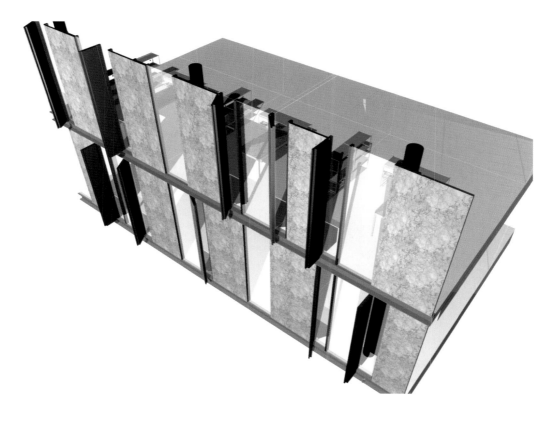

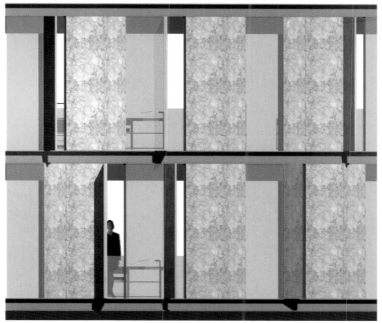

This drawing of the façade shows the succession of glass, stone and openings that give the building an animated cadence despite its fundamental regularity.

Preceding double-page: A computer-generated image of the Avenue de France, set on a concrete platform above the railway lines leading to the Gare d'Austerlitz.

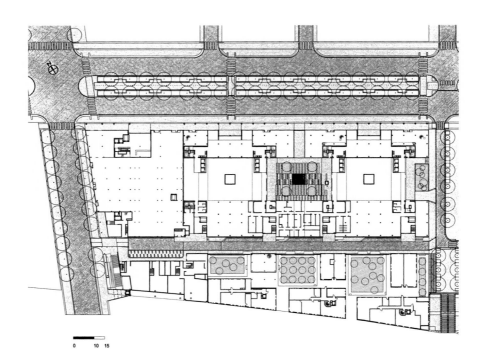

0   10 15

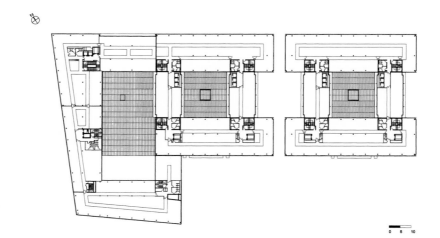

0   5   10

Above:
Floor plans on this page show Viguier's typical mixture of geometric rigor with variations that make for an enlivened space.

Opposite page:
A longitudinal section shows the relationship of the building to the complex underground railway environment. The model gives an impression of the completed design.

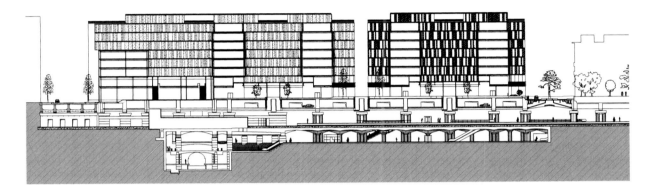

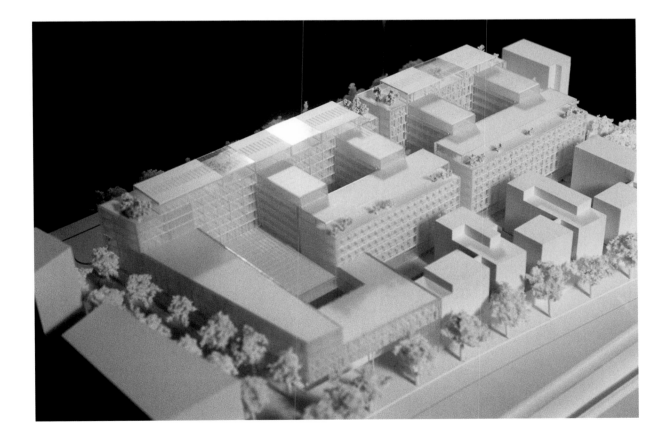

Selected Works

1981/1986

GAZ DE FRANCE RESEARCH CENTER,
La Plaine Saint-Denis
Winning competition entry and
completed project
Client: Gaz de France, Research and
New Technologies Division
Architects: Jean-Paul Viguier and
Jean-François Jodry et Associés
Project architect: Jean-Pierre Marielle
Project team: Patrick Charoin, Dominique
Guion, Jean-Vincent Rischard, Siegfried
Schulz, Vittorio Pisu
Rendering: John Camm
MEP: Seri Renault ingénierie
Program: Offices, IT premises, testing labs
and industrial test buildings, workshops
and warehouses
Budget: FRF 176 million

1986/1987

MÉTROPOLE 19 BUILDING,
Rue d'Aubervilliers,
Paris (19th arrondissement)
Winning competition entry and
completed project
Recipient of the Equerre d'Argent prize
awarded by *Le Moniteur* in October 1988
(special mention)
Client: GA
Architects: Jean-Paul Viguier and
Jean-François Jodry et Associés
Project team: Régis Masson,
Patrick Charoin, Andrès Larrain
MEP: OMEGA
Program: 20,000m2 of industrial premises

1989/1992

C3D HEADQUARTERS,
Boulogne-Billancourt
Designed and completed project
Client: G31
Client's representative: SCIC AMO
Architect: Jean-Paul Viguier SA d'Architecture
Project architects: Michel Raynaud
and Andrès Larrain
Project team: Christian Jensen, Kim
Ritter, John Gibson, Vincent Gilli,
Guillaume Julian, Frédéric Prieur
Consultant : Didier Morax
Model maker: Alain Hugon
MEP: ARCORA (frame and glazing),
SEREQUIP-SIG, CEGEC, Raskin (acoustics),
Light Design Partner (lighting: Jonathan
Speirs)
Contractor: CBC
Program: office building (20,000m2) —
14 levels on square plan with an atrium hub
Budget: FRF 241 million

1990/1992

ESSO HEADQUARTERS,
Rueil-Malmaison
Designed and completed project
Client: Française de Construction
on behalf of Esso
Architects: Jean-Paul Viguier and
Jean-François Jodry et Associés
Project team: Octave Parant, Siegfried
Schulz, Thierry Lacoste
Landscape architect: Kathryn Gustafson
MEP: ELAN
Contractor: Bouygues
Program: Offices laid out in two main
bodies set at right angles, arranged
around a hall grouping the main
vertical circulations
Budget: FRF 264 million

1991/1994

PUBLIC HOUSING,
Avenue Jean-Jaurès, Paris
(19th arrondissement)
Designed and completed project
Client: SCIC AMO — lead architect for
Caisse des dépôts et consignations, SA
d'HLM Travail et Propriété
Architects: Jean-Paul Viguier and
Jean-François Jodry et Associés
Project team: Jean-Claude Antonio,
Christophe Charon, Octave Parant,
Marc Rousseau, Chao Sopsaisana,
Françoise Subra, Laurence Cossard
Rendering: Noé Hernandez
Program: 47 free-rent flats overlooking
the avenue and 37 low income housing
including 8 artists' studios
Budget: FRF 59 million

1992

FRENCH PAVILION,
Expo '92, Seville
Winning competition entry and
completed project
Client: COFRES
Assistant to the client: SCIC AMO
Architects: Jean-Paul Viguier and
Jean-François Jodry et Associés with
François Seigneur and Patrick Charoin
Project team: Mona El Mousfy, Pablo
Lorenzino, Philippe Folliasson, Ivan di
Pol, Manuel da Cruz, José-Louis Pena,
Ghita Zwirner, Catherine Bonnier,
Francesco Zaccaro, Hildegarde Hummel,
Brigitte Van Hoergarden
MEP: ARCORA and SEREQUIP
Site manager: COPIBAT
Quality control: SOCOTEC International
Layout: Didier Onde
Contractor: SAE
Budget: FRF 145 million

1992/2000

ANDRÉ CITROËN PARK,
Paris (15th arrondissement)
Competition held in 1986; park
completed in 1992; viaduct completed in
1998 and Seine waterfront development
completed in 2000
Client: Paris City Council (Department
of parks, gardens and green sites)
Designers of the park: two winning teams —
Jean-Paul Viguier SA d'Architecture
with Alain Provost (landscape architect)
and Patrick Berger (architect) with
Gilles Clément (landscape architect)
Lead architect: Alain Provost
Project team: Jean-Marie Parant, Octave
Parant, Régis Masson, Patrick Charoin
Rendering: François Seigneur
MEP: SGTE
Architect for the viaduct: Jean-Paul
Viguier SA d'Architecture, with
Patrick Charoin
Budget: FRF 300 million
Budget for the viaduct: FRF 23.5 million

1992

CITADINES HOTEL, Berlin
Design studies
Client: SOFAP FUNDUS
Architect: Jean-Paul Viguier SA d'Architecture
Project architect: Patrick Senne,
with Eric Noual
Associate architect in Berlin: Klaus Grunwald
Program: 3-star hotel with 98 rooms
Budget: FRF 80 million

1992

LAW BUILDINGS, Bordeaux
Competition
Client: French Ministry of Justice
Architect: Jean-Paul Viguier SA d'Architecture
Project architect: Cloud Dupuy de Grandpré
Project team: Ivan di Pol,
Octave Parant, Gorgio Colussi,
Francesco Zaccaro, Jean Pascal Verdier
Model makers: Frédéric Forte,
Jean-Louis Goujon
Landscape architect: Laure Quoniam
Rendering: Vincent Alliot
MEP: Beaulieu Ingénierie
Program: A county court, extension to
the National Magistracy School, research
premises and underground parking,
covering 23,500m2.
Budget: FRF 195 million

1992

ÉCOLE DES MINES, Albi/Carmaux
Competition
Client: DRIR (Regional Department
of Industry and Research)
Architect: Jean-Paul Viguier SA d'Architecture
Project architect: Vincent Cortès
Project team: Jean-Louis Goujon, Florence

de Lacharrière, Elisabeth Listowsky
Model makers: Frédéric Forte, Rod Marawi
Rendering: Vincent Alliot
MEP: OCTE Toulouse
Program: A main section comprising two
linear parts: one opaque part housing
administrative offices and teaching
rooms, and one shadowy and airy part
composed of a base forming a terrace
on which the lecture halls rest.

1992/1997; 1997/2001

CŒUR DÉFENSE OFFICE BUILDING, Paris
Competition: 1990
Design studies: 1992/1997
Final scheme: 1997/2001
Planning office: EPAD
Client: Tanagra, advised by Arc 108, the
Unibail Group, Paris
Client's representative: Bouygues Immobilier
Architect: Jean-Paul Viguier SA d'Architecture
Project architects: Andrès Larrain, Ivan di Pol
Project team: Mehdi Jaoua, Christophe
Charon, Yann Padlewski, Sylvie Privat,
Dominique Eyl, Jean-Luc Vignon, Pascale
Meynardie, Roland Malamucéanu,
Jacques Rochery, Hubert Fontaine,
Sandra Eliaszewicz, Nathalie Gaillard
Computer graphics: Christel Catteau,
Anne-Catherine Cozilis
3-D imaging: Sandra Eliaszewicz
MEP: SETEC, AR&C, SFICA
Quality control: CEP and SOCOTEC
Contractor: Bouygues
Façade: Rinaldi Structural
3,000 parking spaces (214,700m2)
Budget: FRF 2.9 billion

1992/1997; 1997/2001

PONT DU GARD VISITOR CENTER, MUSEUM
AND SITE RENOVATION, Nîmes
First design phase:1992
Second design phase: 1997
Client: Syndicat mixte du Pont du Gard
Client's concessionary: Nîmes-Uzès-Le
Vigan Chamber of Commerce
Architect: Jean-Paul Viguier SA d'Architecture
Project architect: Bertrand Beaussillon
Project team: Yann Padlewski,
Jean-Luc Vignon, Alison Rondel
Landscape architect: Laure Quoniam
Site architect: Carré d'Archi, Nîmes
MEP: BET-VIAL (frame), Batelec (flows),
Céaur Houssard (infrastructures)
Budget: FRF 100 million

1993

BABELSBERG GARDENS (filmpark),
Potsdam
Design competition
Client: Euromedien Babelsberg GMBH,
subsidiary of CIP Deutschland
Architect: Jean-Paul Viguier SA d'Architecture
Project architect: Cloud Dupuy de Grandpré

Project team: Octave Parant, Elke
Stumm, Blin Trinçal, Francesco Zaccaro,
Jean-Michel Wahart
Architect in Germany: Peter Seidel
Landscape architect: Alain Provost
Model makers: Frédéric Forte, Frédérique
Desarnaud, Jean-Louis Goujon
Rendering: John Camm
Film director: Pierre Miquel
Program: The site is divided into three
main spaces: the cinema site, the media
site and an open site

1993
ANDRÉ CITROËN GALLERY/PAVILION,
Paris (15th arrondissement)
Designed and completed project
Client: Paris City Council (Department
of parks, gardens and green sites)
Architect: Jean-Paul Viguier SA
d'Architecture, with Patrick Charoin
Project architect: Francesco Zaccaro
Model maker: Frédéric Forte
Program: A gallery/pavilion housing a
number of public facilities, including
a visitor center, public lavatories, café
and bookshop
Budget: FRF 23 million

1993
FRENCH MINISTRY OF FOREIGN AFFAIRS,
Singapore
Competition
Client: French Foreign Office
Architect: Jean-Paul Viguier SA d'Architecture
Project architect Octave Parant
Project team: Francesco Zaccaro,
Ivan di Pol, Frédéric Morel
Correspondent architect in Singapore:
Heak Hock & Partners
MEP: Kinhill Tan
Cost consultant: DG Jones & Partners &
Barton Associates
Program: An embassy comprising a plain,
almost cube-shaped building clad in
white marble
Budget: FRF 25 million

1993
ÉCOLE POLYTECHNIQUE, Lausanne
Competition
Client: Office des Constructions Fédérales
Architect: Jean-Paul Viguier SA d'Architecture
Project architect: Octave Parant
Project team: Ivan di Pol, Francesco
Zaccaro, Blin Trinçal, Frédéric Morel
Associate architects in Geneva: Mrs
Gerber, Mrs. Mentha and Mrs. Renaud
MEP: Philippe Coeur
Program: development of the north
quarter of the École Polytechnique
Fédérale (50,000m2)

1993
EEC CHANCELLERY BUILDINGS, Abuja
Competition
Client: Delegation of the European
Communities
Architect: Jean-Paul Viguier SA
d'Architecture, with Vincent Cortès
Project team: Francesco Zaccaro,
Yann Padlewski, Natacha Soumagnac,
Victoria Rissoli
Computer graphics: Anne-Catherine Cozilis
MEP: Terrell Rooke Associates (frame),
Noble Ingénierie (thermal insulation)
Model maker: New Tone
Program: competition for constructing
EC chancellery buildings
Budget: FRF 200 million

1993
Z TOWER BLOCK
Open research (high-density site)
into housing for the future
Client: Jean-Paul Viguier SA d'Architecture
Project architect: Patrick Senne
Project team: Yves Nguyen, Frédéric Morel
Computer graphics: Christel Catteau
Model maker: Alain Hugon Program:
240m tower block comprising one part of
22 circular levels and four parts of 44m,
each formed of 16 rings stacked conically.
Each unit opens in a way that generates
interior space, responding to issues of
floor space, light and greenery.

1993/1997
GEC ALSTHOM TRANSPORT
HEADQUARTERS, Saint-Ouen
Winning competition entry and
completed project
Client: GEC Alsthom Transport SA
(Alsthom Group)
Architect: Jean-Paul Viguier SA d'Architecture
Project architect: Patrick Senne
Project team: Eric Noual, Marcel David
Computer graphics: Christel Catteau
Model maker: Alain Hugon
Rendering: Vincent Alliot
MEP: SOGELERG
Contractor: Campenon Bernard – EDIF
Budget: FRF 160 million

1993
AL WATANYA OFFICE BUILDINGS,
Casablanca
Winning competition entry
Client: Al Watanya
Architect: Jean-Paul Viguier SA
d'Architecture, with Vincent Cortès
3-D imaging: Yves Nguyen
Model maker: Frédéric Forte
MEP: Beaulieu Ingénierie
Program: a business complex covering
60,000m2, incorporating AL Watanya
headquarters and meeting rooms.

1994/1998
FRANCE TÉLÉVISION HEADQUARTERS,
Paris (15th arrondissement)
Competition and completed project
Client: France Télévision
Architect: Jean-Paul Viguier SA
d'Architecture, with Patrick Charoin
Project team: Christian Chopin, Ivan di
Pol, Marina Donda, Philippe Folliasson,
Francesco Zaccaro, Marcel David, Yann
Padlewski, Sylvie Privat, Yves Nguyen,
David de Castro, Natacha Soumagnac,
Pascal Barhod, Frédéric David
Computer graphics: Christel Catteau,
Anne-Catherine Cozilis
Engineer: Jean Muscat
Decorator: Jean Trindade
Rendering: Vincent Alliot, Natalie Smith
Model makers: Frédéric Forte, Alain Hugon
MEP: ARCORA, SERETE
General contractor: Meunier
Contractor: GTM
Façades: Permasteelisa, Rinaldi, FA
Budget: FRF 653 million

1994/1998
PUBLIC HOUSING, ZAC BERCY,
Paris (12th arrondissement)
Competition and completed project
Client: OPAC de Paris
Architect: Jean-Paul Viguier SA d'Architecture
Project architect: Octave Parant
Project team: Ivan di Pol, Mette Lyng
Hansen, Yves Nguyen, Frédéric Morel,
Roland Malamucéanu
Model maker: Frédéric Forte
MEP: Beaulieu Ingénierie
Contractor: GTM
Program: 52 low income housing
Budget: FRF 28 million

1994
GRAND STADE, Saint-Denis
Competition
Client: Mission Grand Stade
Designers/Constructors: Bouygues/Dumez/
SGE, Jean-Paul Viguier SA d'Architecture,
Ricardo Bofill, Taller de Architectura
Project architects: Vincent Cortès,
Nabil Golham
Project archtects: Octave Parant, Philippe
Bogacz, Nathalie Ringwald, Marie-Hélène
Paoli, Gabor Somssich, Scott Dimit, Tom
Rosenkilde, Jean-François Irissou
Program: a stadium of unprecedented size
in France (80,000 seating capacity for
football/rugby, and 65,000 for athletics)
Budget: FRF 1.5 billion

1994/1997
CONGRESS CENTER AUDITORIUM,
Marseille (seating capacity of 1,200)
Competition and completed project

Client: Marseille City Council (Department
of Large Public Works)
Architect: Jean-Paul Viguier SA d'Architecture
Associate architect: Marie-France Chatenet
Project architect: Bertrand Beaussillon
Project team: Yann Padlewski,
Nathalie Ringwald
Computer graphics: Anne-Catherine Cozilis
Layout: Didier Onde and Sophie Thomas
Acoustics: Aquarecrea
Landscape architect: Jean-Louis Minjaud
Model maker: Frédéric Forte
Budget: FRF 33.5 million

1994/1997
ASTRA FRANCE HEADQUARTERS,
Rueil-Malmaison
15,000m2 of offices and
pharmaceutical laboratories
Competition and completed project
Client: ASTRA France
Assistant to the client: SERETE
Architect: Jean-Paul Viguier SA
d'Architecture, with Vincent Cortès
Project team: Jean-Luc Vignon, Francesco
Zaccaro, Claudia Wetzel, Charles Essers,
Marie-Hélène Paoli
Model maker: New Tone
MEP: Trouvin (flows), Beaulieu (frame)
Decorator: Juan Trindade et associés
Contractor: SAE
Budget: FRF 109 million

1994
PORTE MAILLOT CONGRESS CENTER,
Paris
Competition
Client: Paris Chamber of Commerce
Architect: Jean-Paul Viguier SA
d'Architecture, with Patrick Charoin
Project team: Francesco Zaccaro,
David de Castro, Youssef Ismael
3-D imaging: Derby Informatique
MEP: SETEC
Program: Extension to the Porte Maillot
congress center
Budget: FRF 296 million

1995
CASTEL LAFERRIERE
Designed and completed project
Client: Immobilière Familiale
Project manager: BAPH
Architect: Jean-Paul Viguier SA d'Architecture
Project architect: Octave Parant
Project team: Eric Noual, Mette Lyng-
Hansen, Mehdi Jaoua, Roland Malamucéanu
Computer graphics: Christel Catteau
Rendering: Natalie Smith
MEP: ARCOBA
Contractor: Devilette & Chissadon
Program: 138 low income housing
Budget: FRF 46 million

1995
FEMME-MÈRE HOSPITAL,
Toulouse
Competition
Client: CHU de Toulouse
Architect: Jean-Paul Viguier SA d'Architecture
Project architects: Vincent Cortès,
Octave Parant
Project team: Christophe Charon,
Marie-Hélène Paoli, Charles Essers,
Blin Trinçal, Christoph Denerier
Graphic designer: Cendrine Bonami
Rendering: Didier Ghislain
Model maker: Etienne Follenfant
MEP: SERETE
Program: 220,220 beds for the obstetrics
and gynaecological wards, as well as for
pre- and post-birth care.
Budget: FRF 156 million

1995
LAW COURTS, Melun
Competition
Client: French Ministry of Justice
Architect: Jean-Paul Viguier SA
d'Architecture, with Patrick Charoin
Project team: Francesco Zaccaro,
Mette Lyng-Hansen
Computer graphics: Christel Catteau
Rendering: Mellisa Brown
MEP: Ove Arup (frame and façade),
Trouvin (flows)
Program: law courts (13,000m2)

1995
ESSO HEADQUARTERS –
RENOVATION OF THE RECEPTION AREA,
Rueil-Malmaison
Designed and completed project
Client: Esso SAF
Architect: Jean-Paul Viguier SA
d'Architecture, with Vincent Cortès
Project team: Blin Trinçal, Mette
Lyng-Hansen, Evelyne Roussel
MEP: AR&C, BETI
Contractor: Bouygues
Program: Creation of a rooftop reception
area at Esso headquarters, for executives
and VIP visitors, with a lounge, bar and
dining rooms topped by a foldaway roof.
Budget: FRF 6 million

1995
RENOVATION OF LYCÉE JULES FERRY,
Paris
Designed and completed project
(construction underway)
Client: Paris City Council (Department
of Architecture and National Heritage)
Client's representative: Department
of Schooling
Architect: Jean-Paul Viguier SA d'Architecture
Project architect: Blin Trinçal
Project team: Marie-Hélène Paoli,

Christophe Charon, Charles Essers,
Marcel David
Rendering: Natalie Smith
MEP: Beaulieu Ingénierie
Contractor: SICRA, Léon Grosse
Program: Renovation in four phases
(from 1995 to 2000). Building onto the
classrooms; renovating the kitchens and
canteen; bringing the building in line with
fire safety standards; creating access
points for the disabled; constructing
housing and a car park; renovating the
interior and exterior.
Budget: FRF 80 million

1995
MEDIA THEME PARK, Babelsberg
Competition
Client: Euromedien Babelsberg
Task: undertaking a planning study for
the media theme park in Babelsberg
Architect: Jean-Paul Viguier SA d'Architecture
Project architect: Bertrand Beaussillon
Project team: Guita Maleki, Ingrid Schmid,
Rahim Hachempour, Frédéric Morel
Model maker: Frédéric Forte
Program: offices, hotel and cinema

1995
MEDIEN HÖFE, Ufa-Studios,
Babelsberg
Design studies
Client: CAD
Architect: Jean-Paul Viguier SA d'Architecture
Project architect: Bertrand Beaussillon
Project team: Guita Maleki
MEP: GA/ SCICMA ROOS
Program: 16,700m2 of premises
for the film industry
Budget: FRF 120 million

1996
EDF OFFICES
Winning competition entry
(construction underway)
Client: EDF/GDF
Architect: Jean-Paul Viguier SA d'Architecture
Project architect: Ivan di Pol
Project team: Blin Trinçal, Frédéric Morel,
Sylvie Privat, David Cisar, Andrès Larrain,
Graphic designer: Cendrine Bonami
Rendering: Natalie Smith
Model maker: Etienne Follenfant
MEP: SETEC
Program: 6,700m2 of offices
Budget: FRF 66 million

1996
CB 10, PROJECT 3, La Défense
Design studies
Client: SNC Cœur Défense
Architect: Jean-Paul Viguier SA
d'Architecture, with Patrick Charoin
Project architects: Andrès Larrain,

Ivan di Pol, Bertrand Beaussillon
Project team: Yann Padlewski,
Sylvie Privat, Frédéric Morel,
Christophe Charon, Dominique Eyl
Model maker: Etienne Follenfant
MEP: SETEC
Program: design scheme for two office
blocks at La Défense

1997
TONG JI UNIVERSITY FRANCO-CHINESE
CENTER, Shanghai
Design and construction (in study phase)
Client: University of Tong Ji/Ecole
Nationale des Ponts et Chaussées
Architect: Jean-Paul Viguier SA
d'Architecture, with Patrick Charoin
Project architects: Ivan di Pol, Sylvie Privat
Associate architects: Institute of
Architecture, University of Tong Ji
Model maker: Alain Hugon
MEP: SETEC
Budget: FRF 180 million

1997/2002
MEDIA CENTER, Reims (6,500m2)
Winning competition entry
(construction underway)
Client: Reims City Council
Architect: Jean-Paul Viguier SA d'Architecture
Project architect: Patrick Senne
Project team: Marcel David,
Frédéric Morel
Computer graphics: Christel Catteau
MEP: SERETE construction, ARCORA
Cost consultant: Delporte
Aumont Laigneau
Acoustics: Capri Acoustique
Model maker: Jean-Claude Gouerec
Rendering: Vincent Alliot
Budget: FRF 58.5 million

1997
FRENCH SCHOOL, Frankfurt
Competition
Client: French Foreign Office
Architect: Jean-Paul Viguier SA
d'Architecture, with Vincent Cortès
Project team: Yann Padlewski, François
Drocourt, Alison Rondel, David Cisar,
Christoph Denerier
Associate architect: Hervé Nourissat
Rendering: Didier Ghislain
Graphic designer: Cendrine Bonami-
Redler
Model maker: Etienne Follenfant
MEP: SERETE Construction
Program: nursery school (one floor);
primary school (two floors)
Budget: FRF 70 million

1997
119 FLATS, ZAC LA BOISSIERE,
Rosny s/Bois
Designed and completed project
(construction underway)
Client: Capri Résidences
Architect: Jean-Paul Viguier SA d'Architecture
Project architect: Octave Parant
Project team: David Cisar, Patrick Tavernier
Rendering: Vincent Alliot
MEP: EUROTEC
Contractor: Devilette & Chissadon
Program: 119 flats
Budget: FRF 30.8 million

1997
ARCHE DE MARENGO MULTIMEDIA
LIBRARY, Toulouse
Competition
Client: Toulouse City Council
Architect: Jean-Paul Viguier SA d'Architecture
Project architect: Bertrand Beaussillon
Project team: Michel Sebald, Octave
Parant, Yann Padlewski, Christophe
Charon, Dominique Eyl, Frédéric Morel,
Marie-Hélène Paoli, Sylvie Privat
Associate architect: LCR Architecture,
Toulouse
Computer graphics: Christel Catteau
MEP: BETEM/Trouvin
Acoustics: Capri Acoustique
Rendering: Didier Ghislain
Program: Capitalizing on the prime site of
the multimedia library, centrally located
on one of the city's main avenues. The
aim is to re-forge links with one of the
finest principles in French city planning,
namely creating long views broken up
by buildings. The arch forms an inverse
U, in line with the underpinning
architectural concept.
Budget: FRF 185 million

1997
WORLD TRADE AND EXHIBITION CENTER,
Zhuhai
Design studies
Client: Universal Investments Europe
Architect: Jean-Paul Viguier SA
d'Architecture, with Vincent Cortès
Project architect: Léa Xu
Associate architect: Olivier Vidal
Programming: CER Programmation
Technical advisers: IGAPE, Agence Grenot,
Bruno Cortial
Video: Générique Production
MEP: Patrice Elluin Igape
Program: World trade and exhibition
center covering 5,000,000m2 built on
reclaimed land (protected by a dyke) at
the far end of the future bridge linking
Hong Kong to China.

1997
MASTERPLAN FOR A NEW TOWN,
Bandar Nusajaya
Competition (design studies underway)
Client: Prolink Development SDN BHD.
Architect: Jean-Paul Viguier SA d'Architecture
Project architects: Octave Parant, Régis
Masson, Ivan di Pol, Andrès Larrain,
Blin Trinçal, François Drocourt, Rachel
Rodrigues Malta
Project team: Léa Xu, Francesco Zaccaro,
Dominique Eyl, Marie-Hélène Paoli
Computer graphics: Christel Catteau
Rendering: Natalie Smith
Model maker: Frédéric Forte
MEP: OPUS, Malaysia
Contractor: United Engineers
Program: "Conceptual master plan" for a
new town of 10,861 ha (on a virgin site)
for 650,000 inhabitants. The plan blends
with the contours of the surroundings
and contains urban shapes modelled
directly on Parisian forms.

1997
MULTIMEDIA COMPLEX AND HOUSING,
Bagnolet
Competition
Client: S.I.D.E.C (Société d'Ingéniérie
et de Développement Economique)
Architect: Jean-Paul Viguier SA d'Architecture
Project architect: Ivan di Pol
Project team: Andrès Larrain, Francesco
Zaccaro, Dominique Eyl, Frédéric Morel
Computer graphics: Christel Catteau,
Anne-Catherine Cozilis
MEP: BERIM
Program: multimedia library covering
2,500m2, plus flats and underground
car park (3,000m2), located in the
town center
Budget: FRF 50 million

1997
DUPLEIX ARCADE,
Paris (15th arrondissement)
Designed and completed project
(construction underway)
Client: SEMEA XV
Architect: Jean-Paul Viguier SA
d'Architecture, with Patrick Charoin
Project architect: Francesco Zaccaro
Computer graphics: Anne-Catherine Cozilis
Model maker: Frédéric Forte
MEP: AR&C
Contractor: CBMS Entreprise
Program: Pedestrian arcade
Budget: FRF 6 million

1997/2002
CARRÉ SÉNART SHOPPING CENTER,
Melun-Sénart
Designed and completed project
(construction underway)

Client: Espace Expansion
Architect: Jean-Paul Viguier SA
d'Architecture, with Vincent Cortès
Project architect: Jean Luc Vignon
Project team: Yann Padlewski, François
Drocourt, Sandra Eliaszewicz, Natacha
Soumagnac, Alison Rondel, Christophe
Charon, Marie Hélène Paoli, Dominique Eyl
3-D imaging: Cédric Lane, Atelier Mesh
Model maker: Frédéric Forte/Maquette et Cie
MEP: Générale de Projets/NEGRU/
Barbanel/AR&C
Interior development: Interfaces/
BDG MC CALL
Budget: FRF 450 million

1998/2002
SOFITEL HOTEL, Chicago
Winning competition entry
(construction underway)
Client: Accor, North America,
Constructa NY
Architect: Jean-Paul Viguier SA
d'Architecture, with Patrick Charoin;
Viguier/Teng joint venture
Project team: Blin Trinçal, Marina Donda,
Frédéric Morel, Marie-Hélène Paoli
Model maker: Frédéric Forte,
Jean-Claude Gouerec
MEP: Teng & Associates, Chicago
Budget: US $55 million (1998 value)

1998
DEUTSCHE POST HEADQUARTERS, Bonn
International competition
Client: Deutsche Post AG
Architect: Jean-Paul Viguier SA
d'Architecture, with Vincent Cortès
Project team: Léa Xu, Marie-Louise
Von Baden, David Cisar, Frédéric Morel,
Dominique Eyl
Program: 50,000m2 of offices and
conference rooms

1998
NEW HEAD QUARTERS FOR THE
HUNGARIAN TELEVISION CO.,
Budapest
International competition
Client: Magyar Televizio,
Hungarian Television Co.
Architect: Jean-Paul Viguier SA
d'Architecture, with Patrick Charoin
Project team: Francesco Zaccaro,
Frédéric Morel
Program: Television studios, offices and
communal areas, covering 25,160m2

1998/2000
ANDRÉ CITROËN PARK
WATERFRONT DEVELOPMENT,
Paris (15th arrondissement)
Design and development (underway)
Client: Port Autonome de Paris

Architect: Jean-Paul Viguier SA
d'Architecture, with Patrick Charoin
Project architect: Francesco Zaccaro
Program: River Seine waterfront
development in André Citroën Park
(lawn, concourse and enclosure under
the viaduct).

1998
104 FLATS, ZAC BERGES DE SEINE, Clichy
Designed and completed project
(construction underway)
Client: Capri Résidences
Architect: Jean-Paul Viguier SA d'Architecture
Project architect: Octave Parant
Project team: Patrick Tavernier,
David Cisar, Natacha Soumagnac
Model maker: Frédéric Forte
MEP: EUROTEC
Program: 104 owner-occupier flats
Budget: FRF 33 million

1998
PÉRIGUEUX 2010
Planning and development study
for the city of Périgueux
Client: Périgueux City Council
Architect: Jean-Paul Viguier SA d'Architecture
Project architect: Yann Padlewksi, with
Marie Hélène Paoli
Assistants: Nathalie Monge, Elise Arnoux.
Communications and opinion survey:
Optimus/ Infoscopie/Sofrès
Program: Planning and development
study for the city of Périgueux, to be
implemented by 2010. The study was
split into several phases, with ongoing
consultation of the local community.
Phases 1 and 2 were dedicated to
diagnosis and positioning. Phase 3 was
given over to studies and surveys.
Phase 4 was devoted to putting the
scheme down on paper and presenting
the communication tools. Phase 5 was
underpinned by interactive consultation
with the local population. Each project
phase was conducted in close liaison with
the local council team and an advisory
committee grouping everyone who
wished to be particularly involved.

1998
MUSIC ACADEMY, Strasbourg
Competition
Client: Strasbourg City Council/SERS
Architect: Jean-Paul Viguier SA d'Architecture
Project architects: Octave Parant, Léa Xu
Project team: David Cisar, Alison Rondel,
Natacha Soumagnac, Julia Knaak
Local architect: Epigraph Architecture,
Strasbourg
3-D imaging: Sandra Eliaszewicz
Rendering: Vincent Alliot
Model maker: Frédéric Forte

MEP: SIRR Ingénierie/Cabinet Casso/
E3 Economie/Bruit Son Musique
Program: Building a new music academy
for Strasbourg, containing teaching
rooms, a 500-seat auditorium, a library-
mediatheque, communal spaces, offices
and plant rooms, covering 8,400m2
useable floor space.

1998
CENTRAL MARKET QUARTER, Tel Aviv
Winning international competition entry
Client: Tel Aviv City Council
Architect: Jean-Paul Viguier SA
d'Architecture
Project architect: Bertrand Beaussillon
Project team: Yann Padlewski,
Octave Parant
3-D imaging: Sandra Eliaszewic
Associate architect in Tel Aviv:
Yaar Architects Ltd
Project architect: Jérémie Hoffmann,
Project team: Noa Feld, Vadim Litva,
Paul Embus
Graphic design: Zvi Einat
Model maker: Frédéric Forte
Program: Redeveloping the main market
square in Tel Aviv; building a new quarter
in Shouk Sitonai in the city center—
housing (200,000m2), shops and public
facilities.

1998
BOULEVARD VICTOR STAIRWAY,
Paris (15th arrondissement)
Design and construction underway
Client: Paris City Council, SEMEA XV
Architect: Jean-Paul Viguier SA d'Architecture
Project architect: Ivan di Pol
Project team: Francesco Zaccaro,
Sylvie Privat
Model maker: Frédéric Forte
MEP: ARC
Program: Creating a link between the
pedestrian concourse of Boulevard Victor
station and the Rue du Professeur Delbarre
Budget: FRF 3.5 million

1999
BOULEVARD VICTOR CONCOURSE,
Paris (15th arrondissement)
Designed and completed project
(construction underway)
Client: SEMEA XV
Architect: Jean-Paul Viguier SA
d'Architecture, with Patrick Charoin
Project architect: Francesco Zaccaro,
with Ivan di Pol
MEP: AR&C/EUREC
Program: Redeveloping a pedestrian
concourse outside Boulevard Victor
station in Paris, just opposite France
Télévision
Budget: FRF 6.5 million

1999
58 FLATS, ZAC PORTE D'ASNIÈRES,
Paris (17th arrondissement)
Designed and completed project
(construction underway)
Client: SAGI
Architect: Jean-Paul Viguier SA d'Architecture
Project architect: Octave Parant
Project team: David Cisar, Frédéric Morel,
Mehdi Jaoua
Model maker: Frédéric Forte
MEP: BECT
Program: 29 owner-occupier flats and
29 low income housing plus shops and
public facilities
Budget: FRF 35.2 million

1999/2002
BRISTOL MYERS SQUIBB (BMS)
HEADQUARTERS, Rueil-Malmaison
Designed and completed project
(construction underway)
Client: BMS/Bouygyes Bâtiment
Architect: Jean-Paul Viguier SA d'Architecture
Project architects: Patrick Senne,
Léa Xu, Blin Trinçal
Project team: Frédéric Morel,
Olivier Vendeville, Sharon Adamco,
Ariane Hagendorf, Marcel David,
Nathalie François, Hubert Fontaine
Computer graphics: Christel Catteau
3-D imaging: Cédric Lane
Model maker: Jean Claude Gouerrec
MEP: GECIBA/IBEX/ANEX
Budget: FRF 210 million

2000/2003
NATURAL HISTORY MUSEUM,
Toulouse
Winning competition entry
(construction underway)
Client: Toulouse City Council
Architect: Jean-Paul Viguier SA d'Architecture
Project architect: Bertrand Beaussillon
Project team: Yann Padlewski, Frédéric
Morel, Marie Hélène Paoli, Marina Donda,
Assistant: Lionel Lacombe
Site architect: LCR Architecture
3-D imaging: Cédric Lane, Benoît Mosset,
Laurent Habsertzer, Atelier Mesh
Museum layout: Xavier Leroux Cauche
Landscape architect: Alain Provost
MEP: BETEM
Program: Renovating the Natural History
Museum — revamping the existing
buildings (2,500m2) and constructing
a new building (3,300m2) to link up
directly with the old one; designing
the whole museum layout; creating a
botanical garden
Budget: FRF 95 million

2000
THE 'CUSCADEN TOWER,'
Singapore
Competition
Client: Crawforn Pte Ltd., Singapore
Architect: Jean-Paul Viguier SA
d'Architecture, with Patrick Charoin
Architect in Singapore: Thimothy Seow
Group Architects
Program: tower block containing 54
luxury flats

2000
HAVAS ADVERTISING HEADQUARTERS,
Meudon
Invited competition
Client: Havas Advertising/SARI
Architect: Jean-Paul Viguier SA
d'Architecture, with Patrick Charoin
Project architect: Marina Donda
3-D imaging: Cédric Lane, Benoît Mosset,
Laurent Habsertzer, Atelier Mesh
Model makers: Frédéric Forte,
Jean Claude Gouerec
Program: 5 buildings forming a campus
on the banks of the Seine. 40,000m2 of
offices and 8,000m2 of housing
Budget: FRF 500 million

2000
PANTHEON ASSAS UNIVERSITY (PARIS II)
Competition
Client: Panthéon Assas University
Architect: Jean-Paul Viguier SA d'Architecture
Project architect: Octave Parant
Project team: Michele Circella, Enrique
Santillana
Assistant: Sylvie Gen Yen Song
3-D imaging: Cédric Lane, Atelier Mesh
MEP: ARCOBA/Atélier de Construction
Program: Renovating and extending a
set of existing buildings on the Assas site
and bringing them in line with safety
standards. Designing a library (2,800m2
useable floor space), a 300-seat
restaurant and two 150-seat lecture
halls (30,000m2 useable floor space).
Budget: FRF 125 million

2000/2003
ILÔT M7 OFFICE BUILDING,
Paris (13th arrondissement)
Designed and completed project
(construction underway)
Planning office: SEMAPA
Client: ING Immobilier/SARI
Développement
Architect: Jean-Paul Viguier SA
d'Architecture, with Patrick Charoin
Project architect for the preliminary
design phase: Bertrand Beaussillon
Project team: Frédéric Morel,
Sharon Adamco, Claire Maguin,
Marie-Hélène Paoli, Sylvie Privat

Computer graphics: Anne-Catherine Cozilis
3-D imaging: Cédric Lane, Atelier Mesh
Model maker: Jean Claude Gouerrec
MEP: SARI Ingénierie/OTH
Budget: FRF 408 million

2001
NOVOTEL HOTEL, Le Havre
Winning competition entry
(construction underway)
Client: Accor
Architect: Jean-Paul Viguier SA d'Architecture
Project architect: Francesco Zaccaro
Project team: Octave Parant, Alison Rondel,
Arnould Davadant, Marie Hélène Paoli,
Michele Circella
3-D imaging: Cédric Lane, Atelier Mech
Model maker: Alain Hugon
MEP: Gagneraud
Program: a 3-star hotel (7,300m2
useable floor space) comprising 144
rooms, swimming pool, conference room
and restaurant.
Budget: FRF 52 million

2001
172 FLATS, Créteil
Designed and completed project
(construction underway)
Client: Capri Résidences
Architect: Jean-Paul Viguier SA d'Architecture
Project architect: Michel Sebald
Project team: Sylvie Gen Yen Song,
Catalina Monsavoir, Mehdi Jaoua
MEP: EUROTEC
Program: 80 owner-occupier flats
(5,274m2 useable floor space) and
92 owner-occupier flats (5,724m2)
Budget: FRF 54.6 million

2001
OFFICES, Satory Ouest, Versailles
Design studies underway
Client: UNIMO/CA
Architect: Jean-Paul Viguier SA d'Architecture
Project architects: Octave Parent, Blin Trinçal
Project team: Yann Padlewski, Caterina
Paddoa Schioppa
MEP: OTH/SFICA
Program: offices, covering 31,500m2
on a 35,000m2 site
Budget: FRF 220 million

Biography

Jean-Paul Viguier was born in 1946 in Azas, France. He attended secondary school at Lycée Pierre de Fermat in Toulouse and graduated in architecture (Diplôme d'Architecte) from the École Nationale Supérieure des Beaux Arts in Paris. While at the Beaux Arts he formed one of the founding members of Unité Pédagogique 5 (UP5), together with Jean Bossu and G.H. Pingusson.

In 1971 he received the Arthur Sachs Fellowship for Harvard University, where he obtained his Master's degree of City Planning in Urban Design. While at Harvard he won the competition for redeveloping Montauban city center and returned to France in 1973.

In 1974, he was appointed Assistant Professor at the École Nationale Supérieure des Beaux Arts (Unité Pédagogique 4). He then won the first major architectural competition launched in France after the engineering reform. The brief (1975) was to group the central divisions of the National Meteorological Unit in Toulouse. He was then appointed to the Editorial Board of the review *Urbanisme*, to which he contributed for eight years. He was in charge of a column entitled *Urban Architecture*.

For the following eight years he participated in the development of new towns, constructing several housing schemes and public facilities (in Cergy-Pontoise, Evry, Saint-Quentin-en-Yvelines, and l'Isle d'Abeau). He also helped pioneer bio-climatic architecture and won the competition for Nandy, a solar village.

He founded a collection of books on the modern movement and published books on Eileen Gray, Gabriel Guévrékian and Jean Ginsberg. He also produced a videographic architectural review called *Metope*, with the support of the Institut National de l'Audiovisuel.

In 1981 and 1983 he took part in the Grands Travaux competitions and was awarded first prize by the jury for the Opéra de la Bastille, and the ex-aequo prize for the Tête Défense project.

He was subsequently appointed visiting professor at Harvard and at the Cooper Union in New York.

One year later he won the competition for building a Gaz de France research center in Saint-Denis. He also proposed the design for Euroroute, which was intended to link France with England. The scheme included a bridge and two islands.

In 1986 he won the competition for the André Citroën Park in Paris, in conjunction with Alain Provost, Patrick Berger and Gilles Clément. He was awarded the Grand Prix National Architecture-Ambiance et Energie from the French Ministry for National Infrastructures, for the Gaz de France research center, together with the Equerre d'Argent d'Architecture (special mention) for an industrial building in Rue d'Aubervilliers (Paris, 19th arrondissement). He then received the Grand Prix du Moniteur des Villes for the André Citroën Park.

In 1989 he won the competition for the French Pavilion at Expo '92 in Seville. The same year, he won a competition for redeveloping Pont du Gard—a project that was listed as an historical monument by the President of the French Republic as part of the Grands Travaux projects.

In 1993, the Berlin-based Aedes gallery staged an exhibition on the works of Jean-Paul Viguier, following his winning competition entry for the World Trade Center in Düsseldorf. After this he was entrusted with the Babelsberg film studio project in Potsdam.

He was elected member of the French Academy of Architecture and was appointed member of the Commission Nationale Supérieure des Monuments Historiques by the French Minister of Culture.

In November 1994 he won the competition for the future headquarters of France Télévision in Paris—a symbolically significant building designed to house France 2, France 3, France Espace and France Télévision.

In December 1994, he was awarded the Order of Arts and Literature by the French Minister of Culture. The same year, he won the competition for the headquarters of GEC Alsthom Transport at Saint-Ouen and was voted winner of the competition for the headquarters of the Swedish pharmaceutical firm Astra France at Rueil-Malmaison (for which he received the Business Week/Architectural Record 1999 prize awarded by the American Institute of Architecture). He also won the competition for the extension to the Parc Chanot congress center in Marseille (1,200-seat auditorium).

In 1997 he bolstered his international renown by undertaking design studies for the Franco-Chinese Center of the Tong Ji University, the masterplan of the new town of Bandar Nusajaya (650,000 inhabitants), commissioned by Prolink in Malaysia, and design studies for the world trade and exhibition center in

Zuhai, China. Meanwhile, in France, his competition scheme for the multimedia library in Reims (opposite the cathedral) was voted winning entry. The same year he was awarded the French National Order of Merit.

In 1998, he won the competition for Sofitel Hotel in Chicago, U.S.A. (415 rooms) commissioned by Accor North America, and launched construction of Cœur Défense in Paris La Défense (190,000 m2) containing offices, a museum and shops, commissioned by Unibail/Tanagra.

In 1999 he built a number of housing schemes in Paris, Créteil and Clichy and designed several office headquarters in Rueil and Issy. He launched construction of Carré Sénart shopping center (100,000 m2 of shops , a 16-theater cinema complex and car parks, commissioned by Espace Expansion). He also designed the winning scheme for the BMS (Bristol Myers Squibb)/UPSA headquarters at Rueil-Malmaison, for which he started design studies later that year. He was subsequently appointed Chairman of the French Academy of Architecture, Honorary Professor of the University of Tong Ji, Shanghai, China, and Associate Member of the A.I.A. (American Institute of Architecture).

In 2000 he won the competition for restructuring the Natural History Museum in Toulouse. He also began design studies on 50,000 m2 of shops and offices (block M7, commissioned by ING Immobilier) as part of the Seine Rive Gauche development plan. He was then appointed Officer of the Order of the Arts and Literature. He received the special prize awarded by the Union of Architects of Russia, the Gold Medal of the Union and the Inter-arch Silver Medal at the international Architecture Triennial held in Sofia, Bulgaria, for the Citroën Park in Paris.

In 2001, he won a competition for designing a Novotel Hotel (144 rooms) at Le Havre, commissioned by the Accor Group, and began design studies for 31,500 m2 of offices at Satory (Versailles), commissioned by Unimo/CA.

In May 2001 he was appointed Honorary Fellow of the American Institute of Architects (FAIA).

Jean-Paul Viguier SA d'Architecture
16 Rue du Champ de l'Alouette
75013 Paris
Tel: +33 1 44 08 62 00
Fax: +33 1 44 08 62 02
www.viguier.com
e.mail jpviguier@viguier.com

Selected Bibliography

General

"Jean-Paul Viguier," *Urbanisme*, No. 207, Paris, July 1985, pp. 56–57.

Hervaux Yves, "Un bus un architecte — L'architecture entre dans la ville," *Le Quotidien de Paris*, No. 3216, Paris, 22 March 1990, pp. 24–25.

Hervaux Yves, "Architecture : quand Paris se met en Seine," *Le Quotidien de Paris*, No. 3224, Paris, 31 March/ 1 April 1990, pp. 20–21.

"Invitation au voyage," *Edition Carte Segrete*, 1991.

Edelmann Frédéric and de Roux Emmanuel, "Un palmarès de l'audace architecturale," *Le Monde*, Paris, 16 April 1992, p. 28.

Safran Emmanuel, "Le big business se met au vert," *Match*, Paris, 23 July 1992, p. 10.

Koelher Florence "Espaces publics — Entretien avec les lauréats," *Paris Projet*, No. 30/31, Paris, June 1993, pp. 116–118.

Catalogue de l'Exposition Aedes, Berlin 1993.

Michel Florence, "Dessine moi une tour — revue de sièges," *Archi Cree*, No. 273, Paris, October/November 1996.

Fillion Odile, "Internet la toute petite French connection," *d'Architecture*, No. 70, Paris, November 1996, pp. 6–7.

Allain-Dupré Elisabeth, "Export Jean-Paul Viguier à l'Afex," *Le Moniteur*, No. 4891, Paris, 22 August 1997, p. 19.

Lamarre François, "Les Architectes français se passionnent pour l'export," *Les Echos*, Paris, 19 March 1998, p. 52.

Nogue Nicolas, "Export des résultats encourageants," *d'A d'Architecture*, No. 88, Paris, November 1998, pp. 16–18.

"The French export pioneer architects," *Architecture and Urbanism*, January 1999, pp. 20–21.

Viguier Jean Paul, "Les architectes veulent un public," *Le Figaro*, débats et opinions," Paris, Friday 31 March 2000.

Allaire William, "Fondations Vasarely à Aix, Jean-Paul Viguier architecte de l'invisible," *TPBM* No. 286, Friday 17 March 2000, pp. 16–19.

Allain-Dupré Elisabeth, "Savoir transcender les contraintes — Jean-Paul Viguier," *Le Moniteur*, No. 5041, Paris, 7 July 2000, p.12–13.

Egg Anne-Laure, "Cœur Défense, Paris la Défense, Tour Sofitel, Chicago, Tour Cuscaden Singapour," *Architecte Intérieure CREE*, No. 296, pp. 62–64.

Gaz de France Research Center, Saint-Denis

Loriers Marie Christine, "Un mariage en blanc," *Techniques et Architecture*, No. 379, Paris, September 1988, pp. 65–72.

Maumené Yves, "Des lieux éclairés par la flamme du renouveau," *L'Empreinte*, No. 6, Paris, September 1989, pp. 28–35.

"Centre de recherche du Gaz de France, Recherche gazière, une dynamique de l'innovation," *Sciences et Avenir*, No. 77.

Métropole 19 Building, Paris 19e

"L'image en plus," *Le Moniteur*, No. 4439, Paris, 23 December 1988, pp. 56 and 64.

Vincendon Sybille, "L'industrie de pointe dépose ses valises en ville," *Libération*, Paris, 14/15 January 1989.

Goulet Patrice, "Métropole 19," *Architecture Intérieure CREE*, Paris, January 1989.

Tonka Hubert, "Architecture et Cie — Metropole 19" *Editions du Demi Cercle, Arc et Senans*, October 1990, pp. 1–16.

Tonka Hubert, "Architecture et Cie — Les protagonistes" *Editions du Demi Cercle, Arc et Senans*, October 1990, p. 15.

"Hotel industriel Métropole 19, Paris," *Progressive Architecture*, USA, December 1991.

C3D Headquarters, Boulogne-Billancourt

Lamarre François, "Boulogne-Billancourt, Le grand cube de la caisse," *Le Moniteur*, Paris, 8 March 1991, pp. 62–64.

Fillion Odile, "Sièges sociaux à l'image de l'entreprise," *Le Moniteur*, No. 4589, Paris, 8 November 1991.

Welsh John, "Parisian names remain the same," *Building Design*, England, January 17, 1992, p. 17.

Lamarre François, "Entreprises en Atrium, Le maître cube — C3D Boulogne," *d'A d'Architectures*, No. 22, Paris, January/February 1992, pp. 22–23.

Pousse Jean-François, "Atmosphère d'entreprise, siège de C3D, Boulogne-Billancourt," *Techniques et Architectures*, Paris, March 1992, pp. 67–70.

Arnold Françoise, "Un atrium à la Française, C3D transparence," *Architecture d'Intérieur Cree*, Paris, March/April 1992, pp. 92–95.

"Boulogne, l'Atrium, siège social C3D Caisse des Dépots et consignations," *Totem View*, Japan, July 1995.

Esso Headquarters, Rueil-Malmaison

"Esso une architecture efficace," *Archi News*, June 1992.

Requillart Hervé, "Déménagement, Une nouvelle adresse pour Esso," *Le Figaro* La Défense, 29 September 1992.

Levasseur Géraldine, "Le nouveau siège d'Esso à Rueil, un pari gagné," *France Soir Ouest*, No. 91, ed. Hauts de Seine Nord, 9/22 November 1992.

P.B. "3Rueil-Malmaison et le toit s'ouvre," *d'A d'Architecture* No. 110, Paris, May 2001.

Public Housing, Avenue Jean-Jaurès, Paris 19e

F.M. "Opérations antibruits aux portes de Paris," *Le Moniteur*, Paris, 17 February 1995.

Frerejean Marc and Landauer Paul, "Le logement social, Avenue Jean Jaurès, Paris 19e," *Archi News*, Paris, December 1995, pp. 88–89.

André Citroën Park, Paris 15e

Bossart Evelyne, "Le parc des identités," *Urbanismes et Architecture*, No. 231/232, Paris, October/November 1989, p. 146.

Bayle Christophe, "Zac Citroën, le jardin zen," *Urbanismes et Architecture*, No. 231/232, Paris, October/November 1989, pp. 98–99.

"Park Citroën Cevennes in Paris, Frankreich," *AW Architektur Wettbewerbe*, No. 141, March 1990, pp. 70–71.

Fontenaille Elise, "Le triangle vert," *7 à Paris*, No. 438, 11 to 17 April 1990, pp. 28–31.

V.B., "Parc Citroën 2 + 2 = 1," *L'Homme et l'Architecture*, No. 3, June 1990, pp. 20–21.

Fillion Odile, "Parc Citroën, la nature à Paris," *Le Moniteur*, Paris, 9 October 1992, pp. 80–82.

Joffroy Pascale, "Le Parc André Citroën," *Le Moniteur Architecture AMC*, No. 36, Paris, November 1992, pp. 31–35.

Edelman Frédéric, "Paris, le Jardin des Mystères," *Le Monde*, Paris, 13/14 December 1992, pp. 21 and 24.

Ellis Charlotte, "Parc André Citroën, The rage in Paris," *P/A*, October 1992.

"Espaces publics — Deux nouveaux parcs à Paris" *Paris Projet*, No. 30/31, Paris, June 1993, pp. 90–97, 99.

"Paris, lecture d'un jardin," *Pays de France*, No. 11, July/August 1993, pp. 30–35.

Vanier Thomas, "Critique non parallel parking, two divergent approaches to Urban Parks in Paris — Parc André Citroën," *Landscape Architecture*, Vol 83, No. 4, USA, April 1993.

"Gardening," *The Sunday Times*, London, January 22, 1995.

"Le Parc André Citroën," *Nikkei Construction*, Japan, 2 October 1995, pp. 62–66.

"…Und täglich küsst der Märchenprinz", *Wohnen*, Austria, January 1996, pp. 50–54.

M Poullanouec-Gonidec "Le Parc Citroën — un jardin grandiose," *Le Devoir*, Montréal, 2/3 February 2000.

"The New French Garden," *France Magazine* No. 53, Spring 2000.

Plazy Gilles and Symon Alain, "Paris jardins en mouvement — Garden in motion," *Air France Magazine*, No. 40, August 2000, pp. 70–72.

"Parc André Citroën," *Japan Landscape* No. 31, p. 50–61.

"Parc André Citroën," *GA Document*, No. 49, Japan, p. 70–77.

French Pavilion, Expo '92, Seville

Rambert Francis, "Seville : Une belle tour de Babel," *d'A d'Architectures*, No. 2, Paris, February 1990.

Welsh John, "Hidden depths," *Building Design*, 9 March 1990.

Fillion Odile, "Le Pavillon de la France — Séville," *Le Moniteur*, No. 4502, Paris, 9 March 1990, pp. 94–95.

Edelmann Frédéric, "Un pavillon en creux pour Séville," *Le Monde*, Paris, 16 March 1990.

Cano Ana Mercedes, "El pabellon de Francia en la Expo 92 un alarde de potencial tecnologico," *Correo de Andalucia*, Séville, 17 March 1990.

Valenzuela Javier, "El pabellon frances para la Expo 92, muestra del estilo vanguardista," *El Pais*, 18 March 1990.

Contal Marie Hélène, "Séville, enfin," *Architecte Intérieure CREE*, No. 235, Paris, March 1990, p. 17.

"Pavillon français de Séville, 5 projets pour l'exposition universelle de 1992," *Technique et Architecture*, No. 388, Paris, March 1990, pp. 64–69.

de Gravelaine Frédérique, "Expo 92 à Séville le paradis futuriste," *Beaux-Arts*, No. 78, Paris, April 1990, pp. 30–31.

Vincent-Heugas Gilles, "Séville en avant-première," *Panorama du Médecin*, No. 3149, 2 April 1990, p. 34.

Manceaux Nathalie, "A l'Exposition universelle de Séville en 92, l'air et l'eau pour le futur pavillon français," *Présent*, No. 2052, 14 April 1990, p. 6.

Allain-Dupré Elisabeth, "Ciel de France à Séville," *Le Moniteur*, No. 10, Paris, April 1990, p. 5.

Bayle Christophe, "La victoire sévillane des Poulidors de l'architecture," *Urbanisme & Architecture*, No. 236, Paris, April 1990, p. 17.

F.D., "Pavillon haut, à Séville la France veut faire le plein de vide," *Le Point*, No. 917, Paris, 16 April 1990.

Rambert Francis, "La France à Séville,

le grand bleu," *d'A d'Architecture*, No. 4, Paris, April 1990.

R.H.C., "Francia invertira siete mil millones en la Expo 92," *El Correo de Andalucia*, 29 June1990.

"Un espacio de libertad, Pabellon de Francia," *Sevilla Universal — Expo 92 Sevilla*, No. 9, Seville, July 1990.

"Ein Quadrat im Himmel Spaniens," *Das Haus als intelligente Haut*, July 1990.

"El cielo de Francia," *Architectura y Construccion*, 19 September 1990.

Santini Sylvie, "Séville qui va lever le pavillon," *l'Expansion*, No. 412, Paris, 19 September 1991.

Viguier Jean Paul, "L'Architecture du Pavillon," *La France à l'Exposition Universelle, Séville 1992, Facettes d'une Nation*, Flammarion, 1992, pp. 44–56.

"Séville reine du monde — Expo 92," *Match*, No. 2533.

"Francia, oltre la modernita, the French Pavilion," *l'Arca*, No. 59, Italy, April 1992, pp. 38–39.

Roubaud Marie Louise, "Un architecte toulousain pour le Pavillon France," *La Dépêche du Midi*, Toulouse, 12 April 1992.

Mulot Jean Paul, "Un Pavillon France tout en séductions," *Le Quotidien de Paris*, 18 April 1992.

Pousse Jean François, "Pavillon de France, Séville," *Techniques et Architecture*, No. 401, Paris, May 1992, p. 63.

Roulet Sophie, "Pavillon de la France à Séville," *Tostem View*, Japan, No. 33, June 1992, p. 4.

Allain-Dupré Elilsabeth, "Le Pavillon de la France, Séville," *Le Moniteur Architectures AMC*, No. 32, Paris, June/July 1992, pp. 26–29.

"French Pavilion" *Progressive Architecture*, USA, July 1992.

Nicaud Gérard, "Pavillon Français : bilan positif," *Le Figaro Eco*, Paris, 30 September 1992.

Bruschet Jacques, "Jean-Paul Viguier, créateur du Pavillon Français en visite à Nîmes," *La Croix du Midi*, 1 November 1992.

Vitta Maurizio, "La performance techno-logica — The French pavilion at Seville 92," *l'Arca*, No. 69, Milan, March 1993, pp. 11–15.

Emery Marc, "Un ciel de France à Séville," *Le Figaro*, Paris, 6 March 1998.

de Gravelaine Frédéric, "Séville, tragi-comédie d'un concours," *L'Architecture d'Aujourd'hui*, No. 269, Paris, pp. 19–20.

Pont du Gard, Visitor Center, Museum and Site Renovation, Nîmes

De Roux Emmanuel, "Un projet minimal-iste pour le Pont du Gard," *Le Monde*, Paris, 5 July 1989.

Hervaux Yves, "Le Gard sur le pont," *Le Quotidien de Paris*, No. 3005, Paris, 19 July 1989, p. 2.

Levreau Didier, "Le Gard redécouvre son pont," *Le Provençal*, 10 August 1989.

Rouge Marianne, "Pont du Gard, musée à ciel ouvert," *Le Moniteur AMC*, No. 3, Paris, July/August 1989, pp. 22–24.

Fillion Odile, "Sur le Pont du Gard," *Le Moniteur*, No. 4473, Paris, 18 August 1989, pp. 41–42.

Decroix Valérie, "Lifting pour le Pont du Gard," *Le Nouvel Economiste*, No. 708, Paris, 25 August 1989.

Chaillet Claire, "Le Pont du Gard, tout nouveau tout beau," *Le Figaro*, Paris, 29 August 1989.

Delaunay François, "Le Pont du Gard — Un pont sur un fleuve d'or," *Murs*, April 1990, p. 78.

Bouveret Nelly, "Le Pont du Gard, Jean-Paul Viguier, un message d'avant-garde," *Calades*, No. 111, Nîmes, June 1990.

O.C., "Opération 'média' à Nîmes et sur le site, projet du Pont du Gard : le département reprend l'initiative," *Midi Libre*, 2 February 1991.

Hervaux Yves, "Pour le pont du Gard, un nouveau travail de Romain," *Le Quotidien de Paris*, No. 3491, Paris, 7 February 1991.

Romero Anne Marie, "Pas de péplum au pont du Gard," *Le Figaro*, Paris, 21 March 1991.

Adine Jean Pierre, "Le Pont du Gard fait pont neuf," *Le Point*, No. 1112, Paris, 8 January 1994, pp. 48–51.

Doudies Alain, "L'aménagement du Pont du Gard en perspective," *Le Moniteur*, No. 4883, Paris, 27 June 1997, pp. 123–125.

Doudies Alain, "Pont du Gard nouvelles étapes du projet d'aménagement," *Le Moniteur*, No. 4900, Paris, 24 October 1997, p. 180.

Doudies Alain, "Pont du Gard appels d'offres en vue," *Le Moniteur*, No. 4922, Paris, 27 March 1998, p. 146.

Dollfus Agnès, "Le Pont du Gard enfin rendu au regard," *Diagonal*, No. 138, Paris, July-August 1999, pp. 25–27.

J.M., "La Renaissance du Pont du Gard," *Air France Magazine*, No. 38, June 2000, pp. 66–76.

Lamarre François, "Le retour à la nature du Pont du Gard," *Les Echos*, Paris, 29 June 2000.

Rambert Francis, "L'aqueduc reprend des couleurs," *Le Figaro*, Paris, 14 July 2000.

de Roux Emmanuel, "Une deuxième chance pour la renommée du Pont du

Gard," *Le Monde*, Paris, 18 July 2000.

Rouyer Rémi, "Requalification d'un paysage," *Architecte Intérieur CREE*, No. 295, Paris, pp. 96–103.

St.B. "Les habits neufs du Pont du Gard," *Connaissance des Arts*, No. 575, Paris, September 2000.

Lamarre François, "Pont du Gard : retour à la nature," *L'empreinte*, No. 50, Paris, September 2000, pp. 10–12.

Vermeil Jean, "Pont du Gard " *d'A d'Architecture*, No. 105, Paris, October 2000, pp. 36–38.

G.D., "Aménagement du Site du Pont du Gard," *AMC*, no. 110, Paris, October 2000, pp. 78–82.

Rouyer R., "Requalification d'un paysage," *AMC*, Paris, October 2000, pp. 98–102.

Loyer Béatrice, "Roma antiqua, semper nova, le Pont du Gard," *Techniques et Architecture*, Paris, October/November 2000, pp. 93–96.

Houzelle Béatrice, "Un site restitué à sa beauté initiale," *Construction Moderne/Cim Béton*, No. 106, 1 trimester 2001, pp. 7–10.

O.V., "Pont du Gard, un aménagement colossal," *Archeologia*, No. 379, June 2001, pp. 4–6.

GEC Alsthom Transport Headquarters, Saint-Ouen

"Gec Alsthom Transport, en avant poste à Saint-Ouen," *Archi News*, December 1995, p. 56.

Colybes Annick, "Gec Alsthom : le pari de la communication d'entreprise," *Les Echos*, Paris, 4 September 1997, p. 42.

Congress Center Auditorium, Marseille

Dupuy Alain, "Le Palais des congrès nouveau est annoncé," *Le Provençal*, Marseille, 8 April 1995.

Public Housing ZAC Bercy, Paris 12e

Cristofaro Florence, "Paris 12e 52 Logements Pla," *AMC*, No. 93, Paris, November 1998, pp. 82–83.

Astra France Headquarters, Rueil-Malmaison

Sabbah Catherine, "Laboratoires Astra France : l'envers du décor," *Architecture Intérieure Cree*, No. 280, Paris, December 1997/January 1998, pp. 100–103.

"Astra France, transparence et clarté," *Archi News*, Paris, July 1998, pp. 40–45.

Lamarre François, "Consensus nordique," *L'Empreinte*, No. 45, Paris, June 1999, p. 10–13.

"The third annual Business Week/ Archi-tectural Record Awards," *Architectural

Record*, October 1999, pp. 104–105.

"Le siège d'Astra France reçoit le prix Business Week/Architectural Record," *Le Moniteur*, No. 5007, Paris, 12 November 1999.

"Business Week/Architectural Record Awards — Good looking, Hardworking," *Business Week*, 1 November, 1999, p. 132.

"Viguier honoré à New York," *d'A d'Architecture*, No. 97, November 1999.

Lamarre François, "L'art du consensus au siège d'Astra France à Rueil Malmaison," *Les Echos*, Paris, 2 December 1999, p. 58.

France Télévision Headquarters, Paris, 15e

Colybas Annick, "La télévision publique opte pour l'architecte Jean-Paul Viguier," *Les Echos*, 15 December 1994.

Rambert Francis, "France 2 et France 3 réunies sur un même site, Quand la télévision cadre sur la Seine," *Le Figaro*, 16 December 1994.

Edelmann Frédéric, "Le choix du projet Viguier pour le siège de France Télévision, la tentation du sandwich," *Le Monde*, Paris, 17 December 1994, p. 17.

Lamarre François, "France Télévision : deux en un," *Les Echos*, Paris, 22 December 1994.

Tomasini Olivier, "Siège de France Télévision 2 + 3 = 1," *d'A d'Architecture*, No. 52, Paris, January/February 1995, p. 16.

"France Télévision entre en scène," *Le Parisien*, No. 15736, Paris, 7 April 1995.

Feraud Jean Christophe, "France Télévison : mise en chantier du nouveau siège," *La Tribune Desfossès*, Paris, August 1995.

Aldebert Bernard, "Un volume de 18.500 m3 sur boites à ressorts," Le Moniteur, No. 4851, Paris, 15 November 1996, pp. 106–107.

Donnaes Philippe and Reinteau Bernard, "France Télévision joue la transparence," *Le Moniteur*, No. 4889, Paris, 8 August 1997, pp. 38–39.

l'Arca2 international, "France Télévision le nouveau siège social à Paris," *l'Arca International*, No. 16, Monaco, September 1997, p. 89.

Ferretti Marc, "France Télévision Réseaux : un système d'information de projet pour la synthèse," *Les Cahiers Techniques du Moniteur*, No. 183, Paris, October 1997, pp. 51–52.

Blin Pascale, "France Télévision : pattes de sécurité pour façade VEC", *Cahiers

Techniques du Bâtiment, No. 185, Paris, December 1997, p. 3.

Guiol Elsa, "Siège de France Télévision : une mini-ville américaine," *Le Journal du Dimanche*, No. 2660, Paris, 21 December 1997, p. 8.

Revel Renaud, "Le médialand de France Télévision," *L'Express*, No. 2434, Paris, 26 February 1998, pp. 66–69.

Allain Dupré Elisabeth, "Siège de France Télévision, Paris XV amarré sur la Seine," *Le Moniteur*, No. 4927, Paris, 2 May 1998, pp. 40–41.

Abrighi Marie-Dominique, "France Télévision un siège pour deux," *Libération*, Paris, 25 May 1998, pp. 46–47.

Rambert Francis, "Les transparences de France Télévision," *Le Figaro*, Paris, 25 June 1998, p. 12.

Edelmann Frédéric, "L'utopie fédératrice de nouveau siège de France Télévision," *Le Monde*, Paris, 9 June 1998, rubrique Culture.

Borde Dominique, "Gouyou-Beauchamps : Tout le monde semble content," *Le Figaro*, Paris, 25 June 1998, p. 12.

Blin Pascale, "La télé en poste sur la Seine," *d'Architecture*, No. 86, Paris, September 1998, p. 36.

Desmoulins Christine, "France Télévision, une image, trois entreprises" *Architecture Intérieure Cree*, No. 284, Paris, October 1998, pp. 81–85.

Caille Jean François, "Paris siège de France Télévision," *AMC*, No. 92, Paris, October 1998, pp. 74–75.

Dana Karine, "Siège de France Télévision," *AMC*, Spécial tertiaire, Paris, November 1998, pp. 22–25.

"Glazing," *Details in Architecture 2, Images*, Australia, pp. 202–203.

Carré Sénart Shopping Center, Melun-Sénart

"Francilia un grand projet," *Média Sénart*, No. 41, Sénart, July/August 1989, pp. 1–3.

Caltot Jean François, "Zac du Carré Sénart démarrage du chantier du centre commercial en 1999," *Le Moniteur*, No. 4901, Paris, 31 October 1997, p. 187.

Félix Frédéric, "Un cœur de ville autour d'un pôle commercial," *Le Moniteur*, No. 5032, Paris, 5 May 2000.

Media Center, Reims

Rambert Francis, "Reims sobre modernité face à la cathédrale," *d'Architectures*, No. 76, Paris, August/September 1997, p. 5.

L'Arca 2 international, "Médiathèque : transparences à Reims," *l'Arca International*, No. 20, Monaco,

January 1998, p. 89.

Lamarrre François, "La médiathèque de Reims : confrontation historique sur le parvis," *Les Echos*, Paris, 14 May 1998, p. 60.

Cœur Défense Office Building, Paris La Défense

G.S., "Le sort de la tour Esso bientôt scellé," *Le Figaro*, Paris, 28 June 1990.

Zennou Albert, "Esso au cœur du réaménagement," *Le Figaro*, La Défense, 24 September 1990.

Hervaux Yves, "Cette tour de la Défense que l'on va démolir," *Le Quotidien de Paris*, No. 3402, Paris, 26 October 1990.

Richard Julie, "Esso Cœur Défense," *Developpeurs*, No. 6, Genevilliers, December 1990/January 1991.

"La torre raddoppiata, a tower and its double," *l'Arca*, Milan, No. 72, Italy, June 1993, p. 18–21.

Vaysse François, "Le projet Cœur Défense sera livré fin 2000–début 2001," *Le Moniteur*, No. 4948, Paris, 25 September 1998, p. 22.

Lamarre François, "Cœur Défense : le profil optimisé des tours jumelles," *Les Echos*, Paris, 15 April 1999, p. 62.

Bietry-Rivière Eric, "Une cité du troisième millénaire," *Le Figaro*, Paris, 17 September 1999, p. 26.

Gally Laurent, "Cœur Défense objectif lumière," *Valeurs Actuelles*, 2 October 1999, pp. 88–90.

"'Salvant Catherine,' Le bureau idéal, beau utile et durable à la fois," *Le Figaro Magazine*, Paris, 23 October 1999, p. 146.

Menard Jean Pierre, "Les façades double peau," *AMC*, No. 101, Paris, October 1999, pp. 76–79.

Echikson William, "Why the air and light are so much better in Paris," *Business Week*, 5 June, 2000, p. 124.

Klauser Wilhem, "Glanzvolles Ende der Zukunft," *Bauwelt*, No. 6/01, Berlin, February 2001.

"Transparence et grands volumes pour bureaux flexibles," *Le Moniteur*, special no., May 2001, pp. 12–13.

Sofitel Hotel, Chicago

"Hotel Sofitel à Chicago : Jean-Paul Viguier lauréat," *Le Moniteur*, No. 4947, Paris, 18 September 1998, p. 7.

Nogue Nicolas, "Export, des résultats encourageants," *d'A d'Architectures*, No. 88, Paris, November 1998, pp. 17–18.

Lamarre François, "La blanche épure du Sofitel de Chicago," *Les Echos*, Paris, 18 February 1999, p. 44.

Gardani Elena, "Un Français à Chicago —

Sofitel Chicago," *l'Arca International* No. 34, Monaco, May 2000, pp. 34–35.

Ilôt M7 Office Building, Paris 13e

"Etudes et analyses — fiche technique," *Estate Consultant*, No. 27, Paris, pp. 6–7.